STUFFED

by
Extended Play

EP Publishing

EP Publishing

ISBN: 978-1-54398-243-5

First Printing – August 2019

For Charles, Berkeley, and Bill,
whose genius inspired us to become cartoonists.

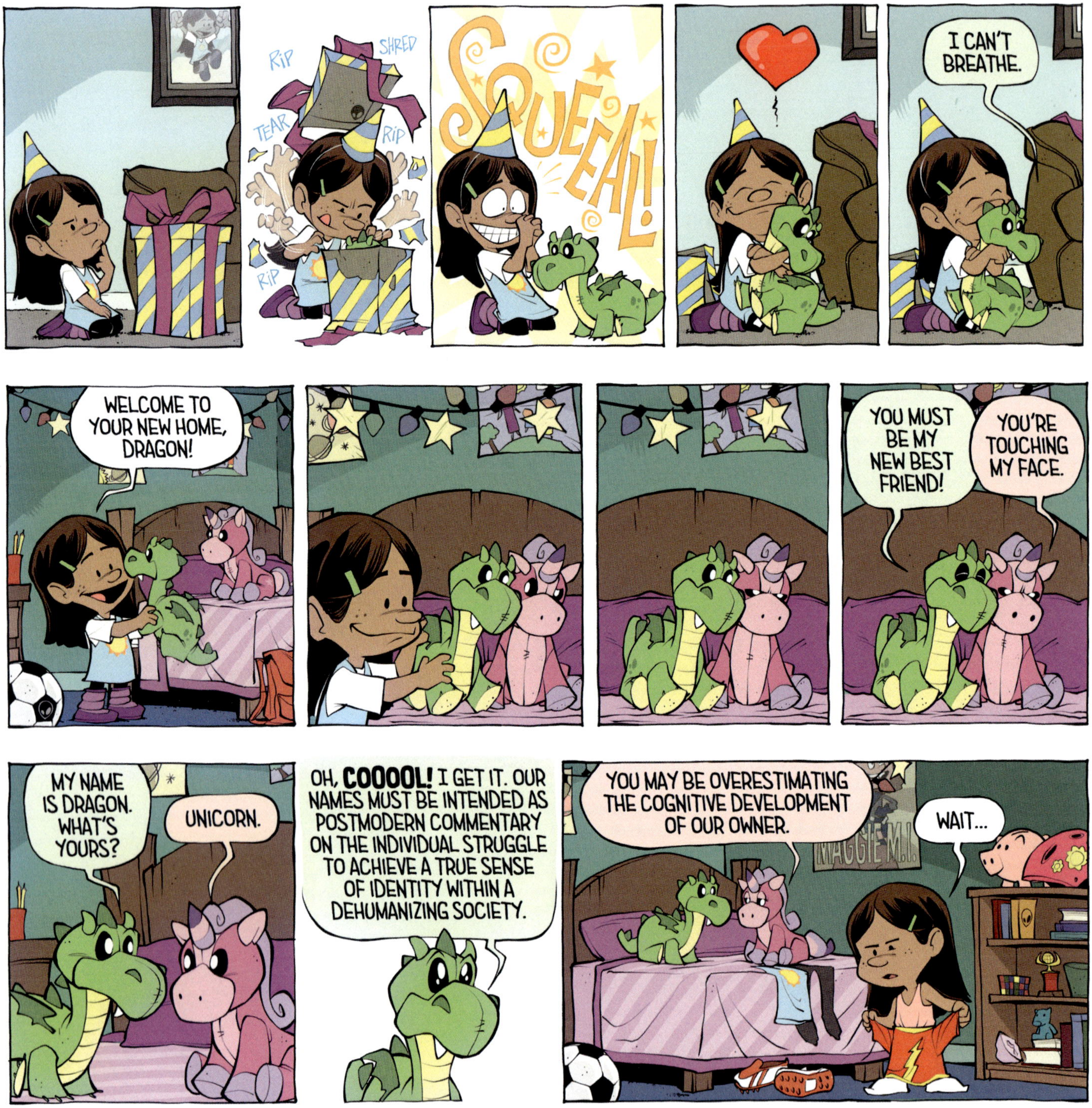
RIP
SHRED
TEAR
RIP
RIP
SQUEEAL!
I CAN'T BREATHE.
WELCOME TO YOUR NEW HOME, DRAGON!
YOU MUST BE MY NEW BEST FRIEND!
YOU'RE TOUCHING MY FACE.
MY NAME IS DRAGON. WHAT'S YOURS?
UNICORN.
OH, **COOOOL!** I GET IT. OUR NAMES MUST BE INTENDED AS POSTMODERN COMMENTARY ON THE INDIVIDUAL STRUGGLE TO ACHIEVE A TRUE SENSE OF IDENTITY WITHIN A DEHUMANIZING SOCIETY.
YOU MAY BE OVERESTIMATING THE COGNITIVE DEVELOPMENT OF OUR OWNER.
WAIT...
MAGGIE M.I.

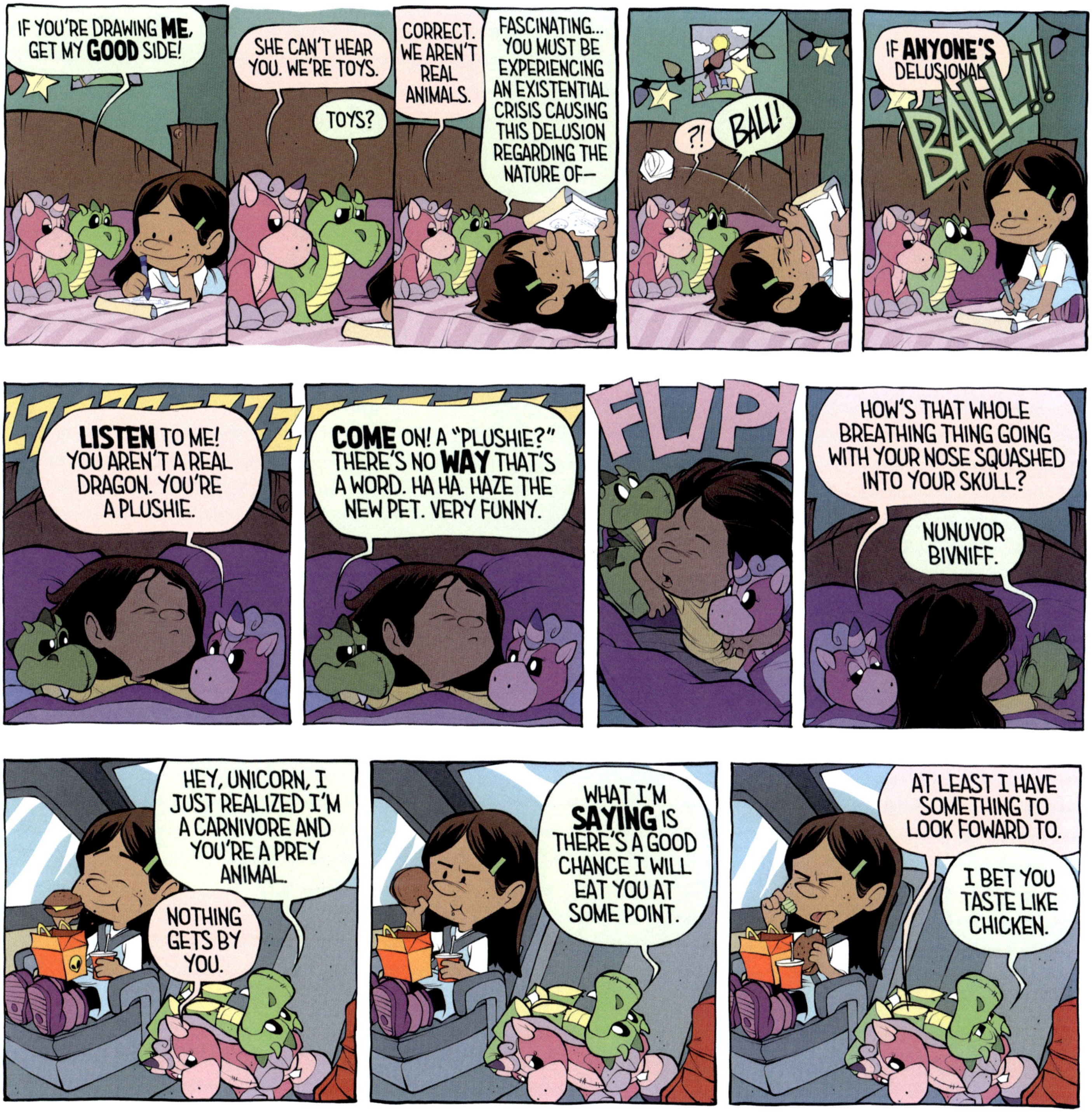
IF YOU'RE DRAWING **ME**, GET MY **GOOD** SIDE!
SHE CAN'T HEAR YOU. WE'RE TOYS.
TOYS?
CORRECT. WE AREN'T REAL ANIMALS.
FASCINATING... YOU MUST BE EXPERIENCING AN EXISTENTIAL CRISIS CAUSING THIS DELUSION REGARDING THE NATURE OF—
?!
BALL!
IF **ANYONE'S** DELUSIONAL
BALL!!!
LISTEN TO ME! YOU AREN'T A REAL DRAGON. YOU'RE A PLUSHIE.
COME ON! A "PLUSHIE?" THERE'S NO **WAY** THAT'S A WORD. HA HA. HAZE THE NEW PET. VERY FUNNY.
FLIP!
HOW'S THAT WHOLE BREATHING THING GOING WITH YOUR NOSE SQUASHED INTO YOUR SKULL?
NUNUVOR BIVNIFF.
HEY, UNICORN, I JUST REALIZED I'M A CARNIVORE AND YOU'RE A PREY ANIMAL...
NOTHING GETS BY YOU.
WHAT I'M **SAYING** IS THERE'S A GOOD CHANCE I WILL EAT YOU AT SOME POINT.
AT LEAST I HAVE SOMETHING TO LOOK FOWARD TO.
I BET YOU TASTE LIKE CHICKEN.

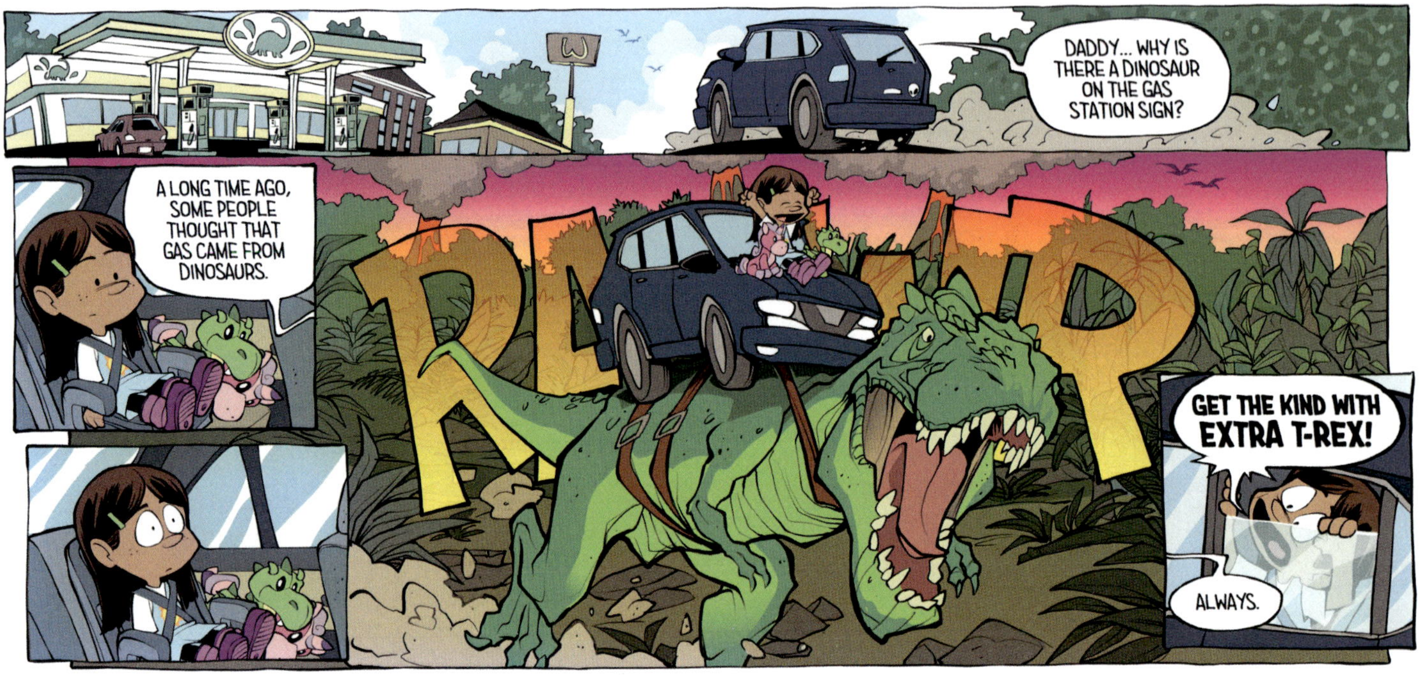
DADDY... WHY IS THERE A DINOSAUR ON THE GAS STATION SIGN?
A LONG TIME AGO, SOME PEOPLE THOUGHT THAT GAS CAME FROM DINOSAURS.
GET THE KIND WITH EXTRA T-REX!
ALWAYS.

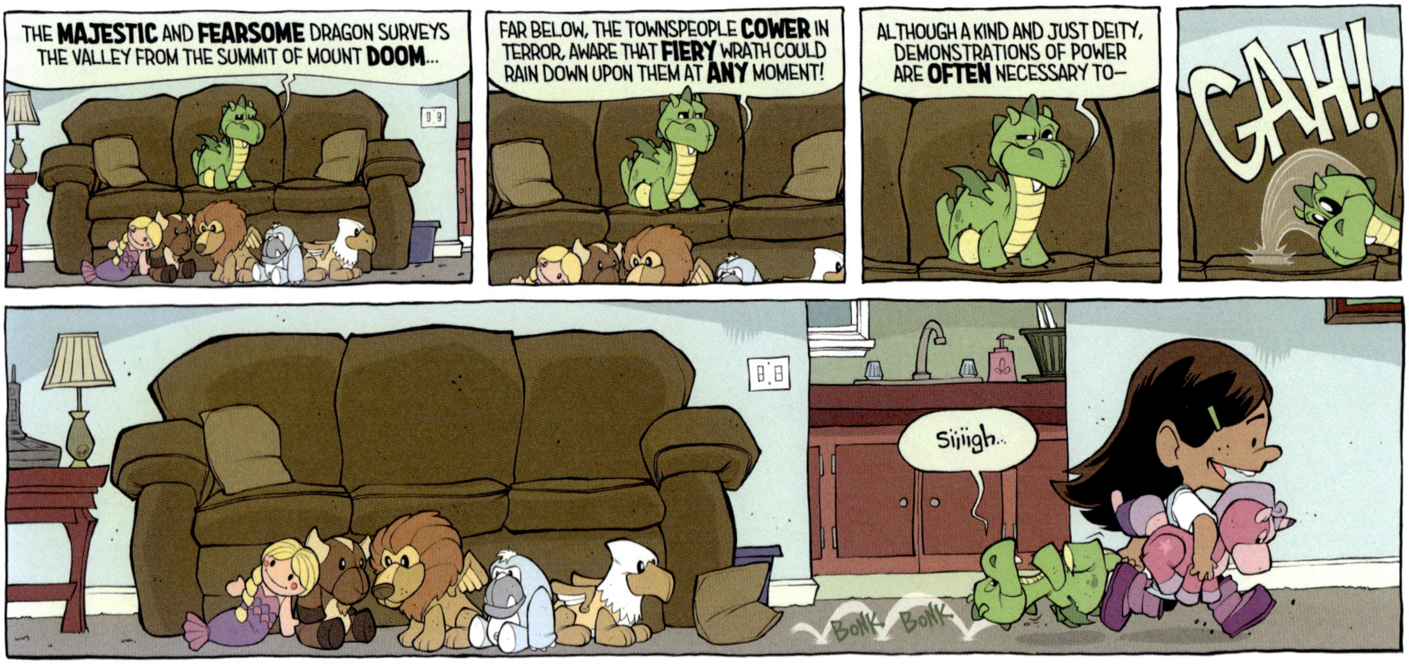
THE MAJESTIC AND FEARSOME DRAGON SURVEYS THE VALLEY FROM THE SUMMIT OF MOUNT DOOM...
FAR BELOW, THE TOWNSPEOPLE COWER IN TERROR, AWARE THAT FIERY WRATH COULD RAIN DOWN UPON THEM AT ANY MOMENT!
ALTHOUGH A KIND AND JUST DEITY, DEMONSTRATIONS OF POWER ARE OFTEN NECESSARY TO—
GAH!
Siiiigh..
BONK BONK

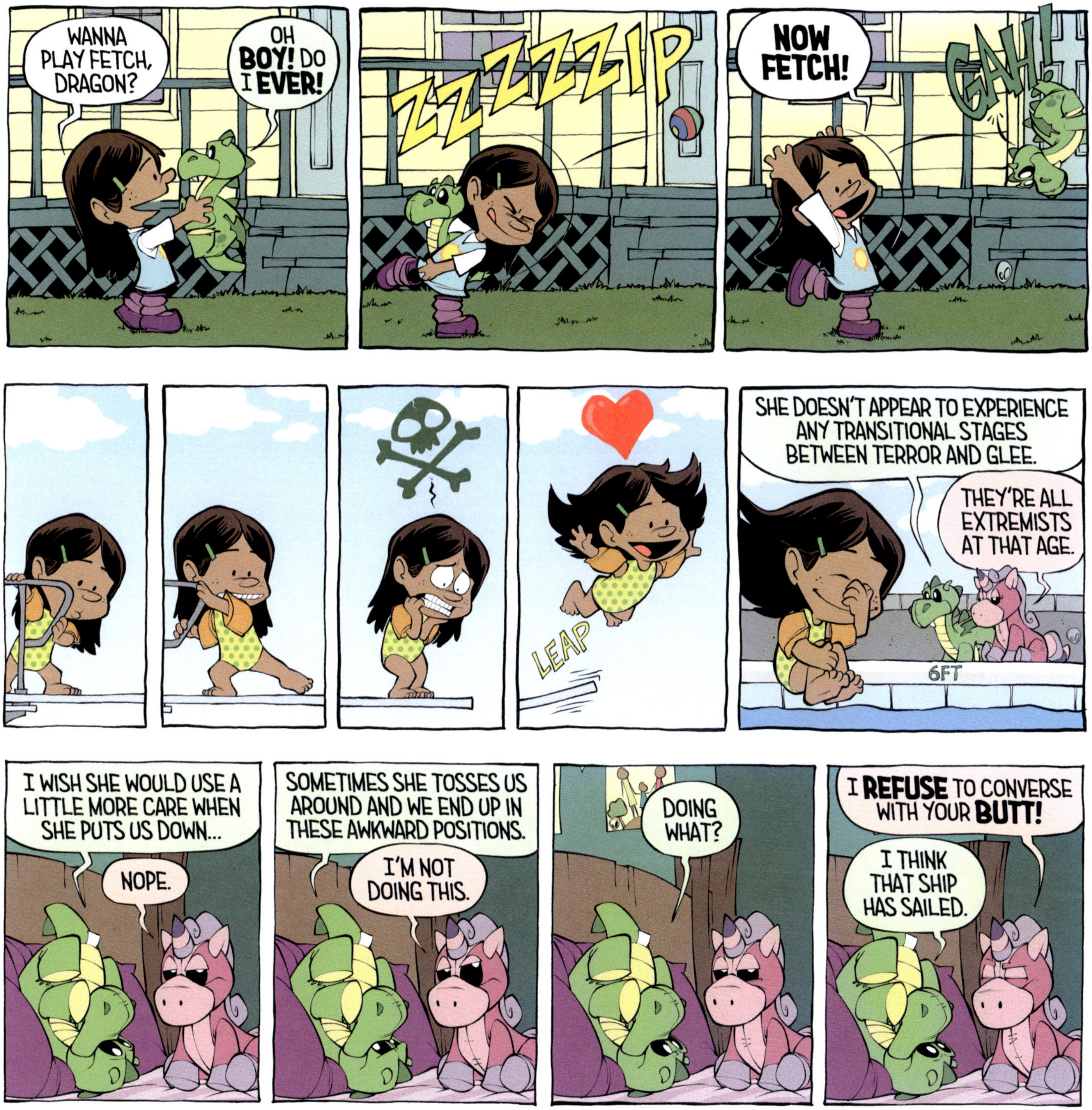
WANNA PLAY FETCH, DRAGON?
OH BOY! DO I EVER!
ZZZZZZIP
NOW FETCH!
GAH!
LEAP
SHE DOESN'T APPEAR TO EXPERIENCE ANY TRANSITIONAL STAGES BETWEEN TERROR AND GLEE.
THEY'RE ALL EXTREMISTS AT THAT AGE.
6FT
I WISH SHE WOULD USE A LITTLE MORE CARE WHEN SHE PUTS US DOWN...
NOPE.
SOMETIMES SHE TOSSES US AROUND AND WE END UP IN THESE AWKWARD POSITIONS.
I'M NOT DOING THIS.
DOING WHAT?
I REFUSE TO CONVERSE WITH YOUR BUTT!
I THINK THAT SHIP HAS SAILED.

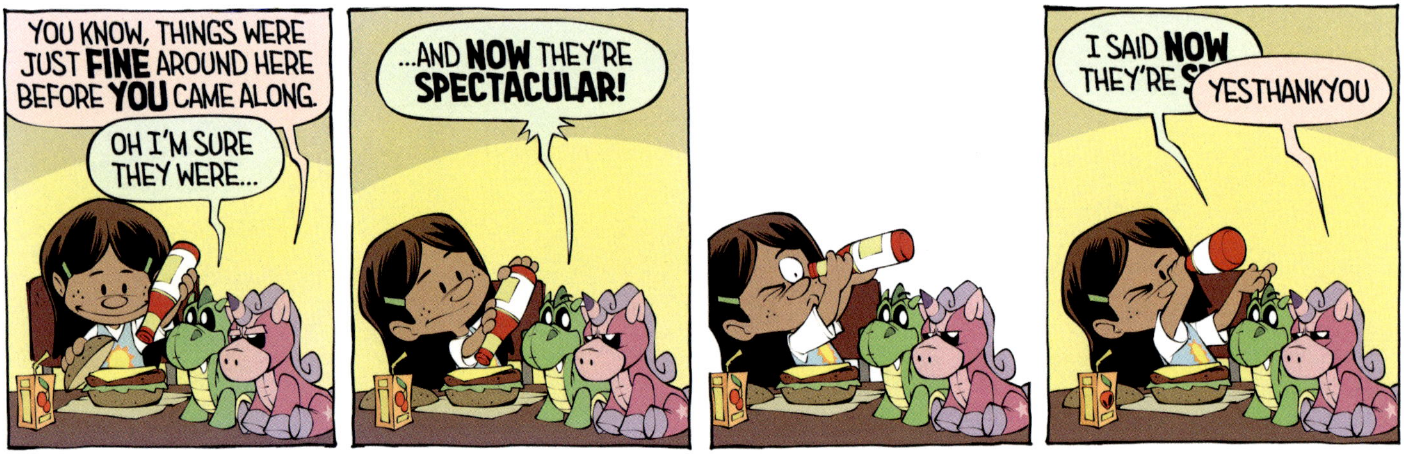
YOU KNOW, THINGS WERE JUST **FINE** AROUND HERE BEFORE **YOU** CAME ALONG.
OH I'M SURE THEY WERE...
...AND **NOW** THEY'RE **SPECTACULAR!**
I SAID **NOW** THEY'RE
YESTHANKYOU

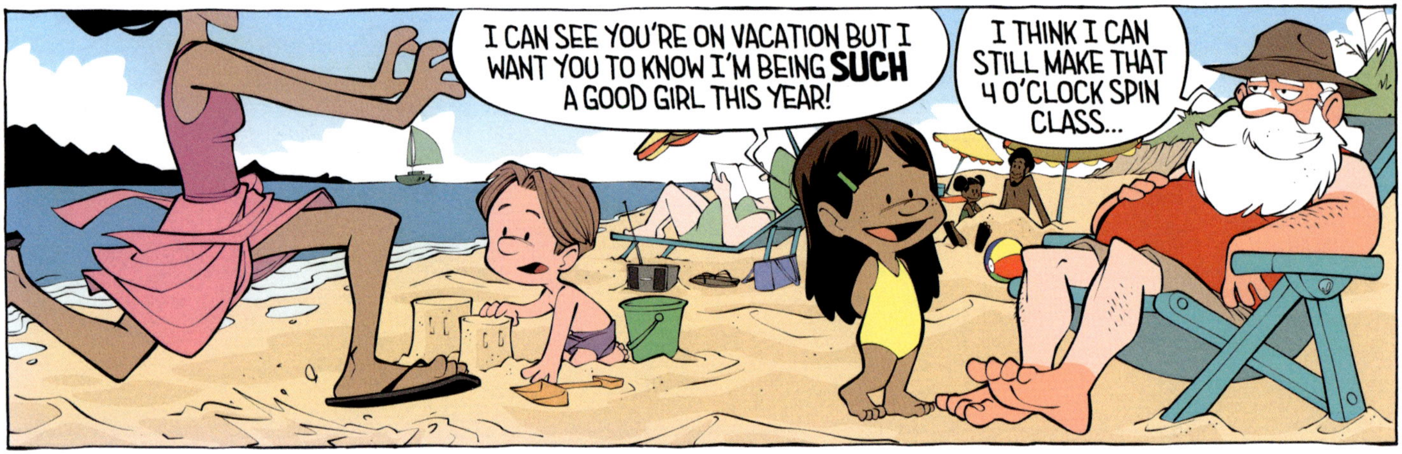
I CAN SEE YOU'RE ON VACATION BUT I WANT YOU TO KNOW I'M BEING **SUCH** A GOOD GIRL THIS YEAR!
I THINK I CAN STILL MAKE THAT 4 O'CLOCK SPIN CLASS...

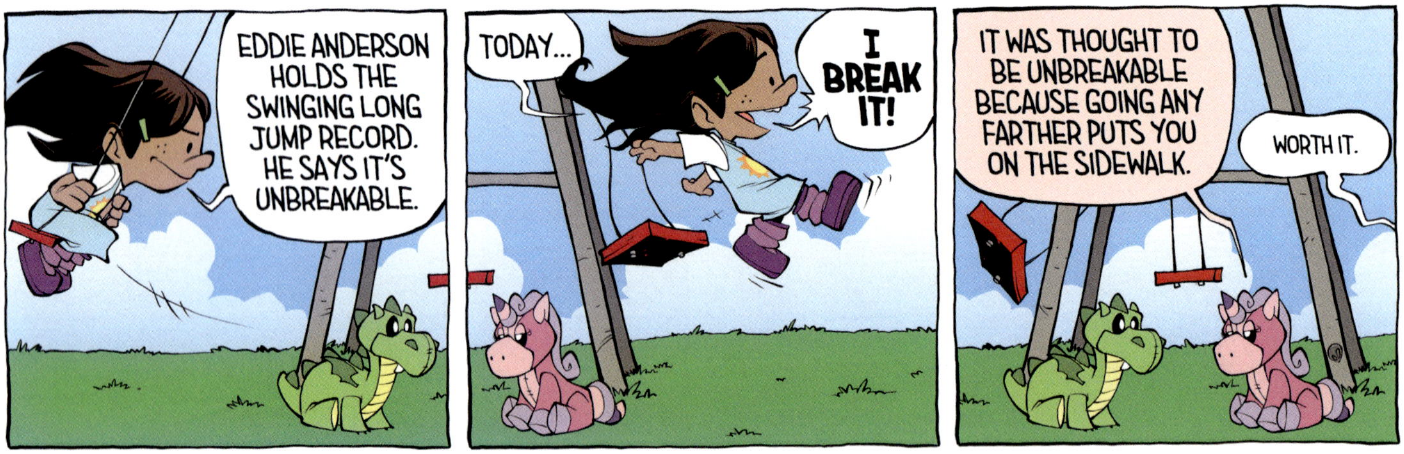
EDDIE ANDERSON HOLDS THE SWINGING LONG JUMP RECORD. HE SAYS IT'S UNBREAKABLE.
TODAY...
I BREAK IT!
IT WAS THOUGHT TO BE UNBREAKABLE BECAUSE GOING ANY FARTHER PUTS YOU ON THE SIDEWALK.
WORTH IT.

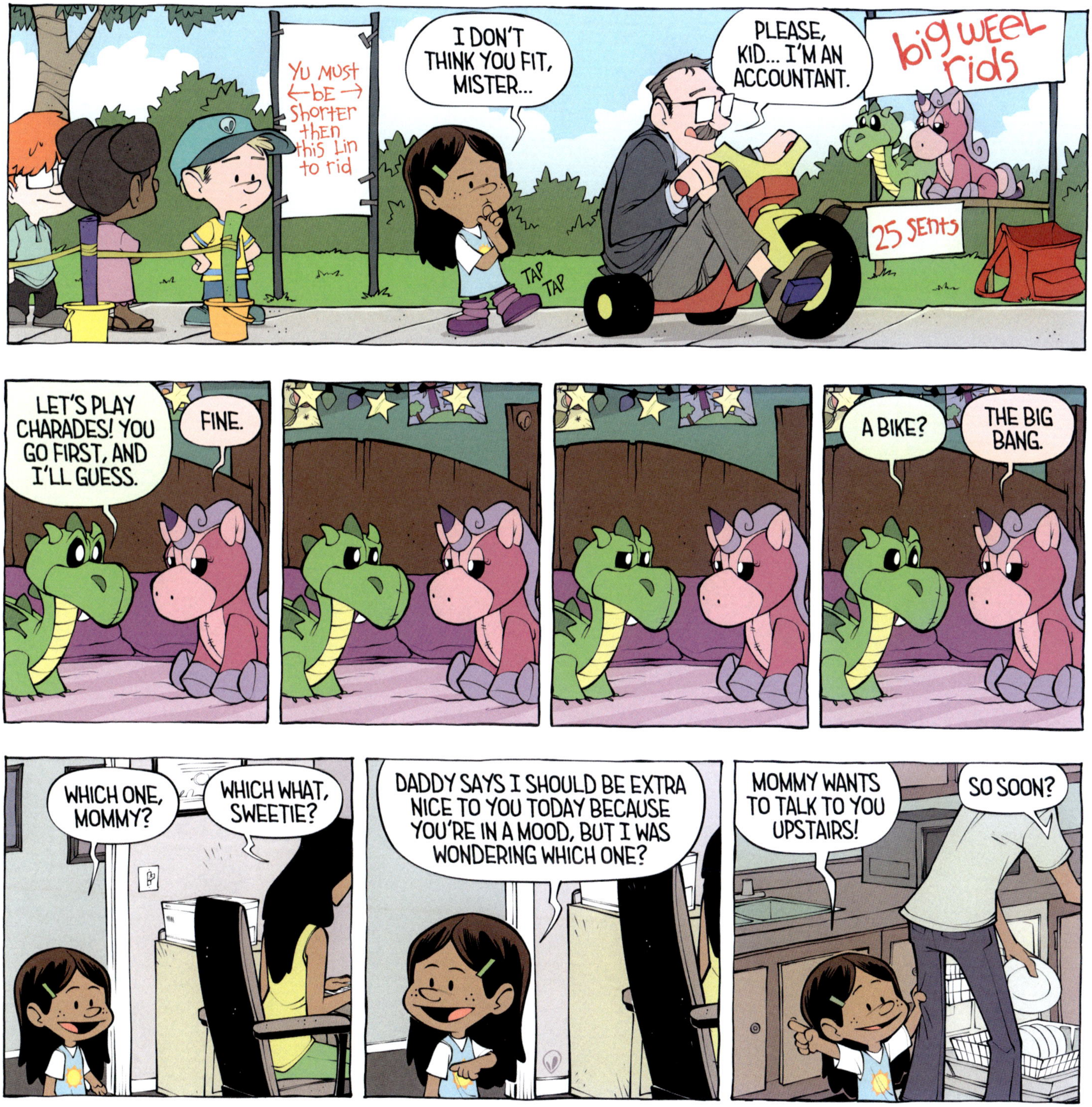

YU MUST
←BE→
SHORTER
THEN
THIS LIN
TO RID
I DON'T THINK YOU FIT, MISTER...
TAP TAP
PLEASE, KID... I'M AN ACCOUNTANT.
big weel rids
25 sents
LET'S PLAY CHARADES! YOU GO FIRST, AND I'LL GUESS.
FINE.
A BIKE?
THE BIG BANG.
WHICH ONE, MOMMY?
WHICH WHAT, SWEETIE?
DADDY SAYS I SHOULD BE EXTRA NICE TO YOU TODAY BECAUSE YOU'RE IN A MOOD, BUT I WAS WONDERING WHICH ONE?
MOMMY WANTS TO TALK TO YOU UPSTAIRS!
SO SOON?

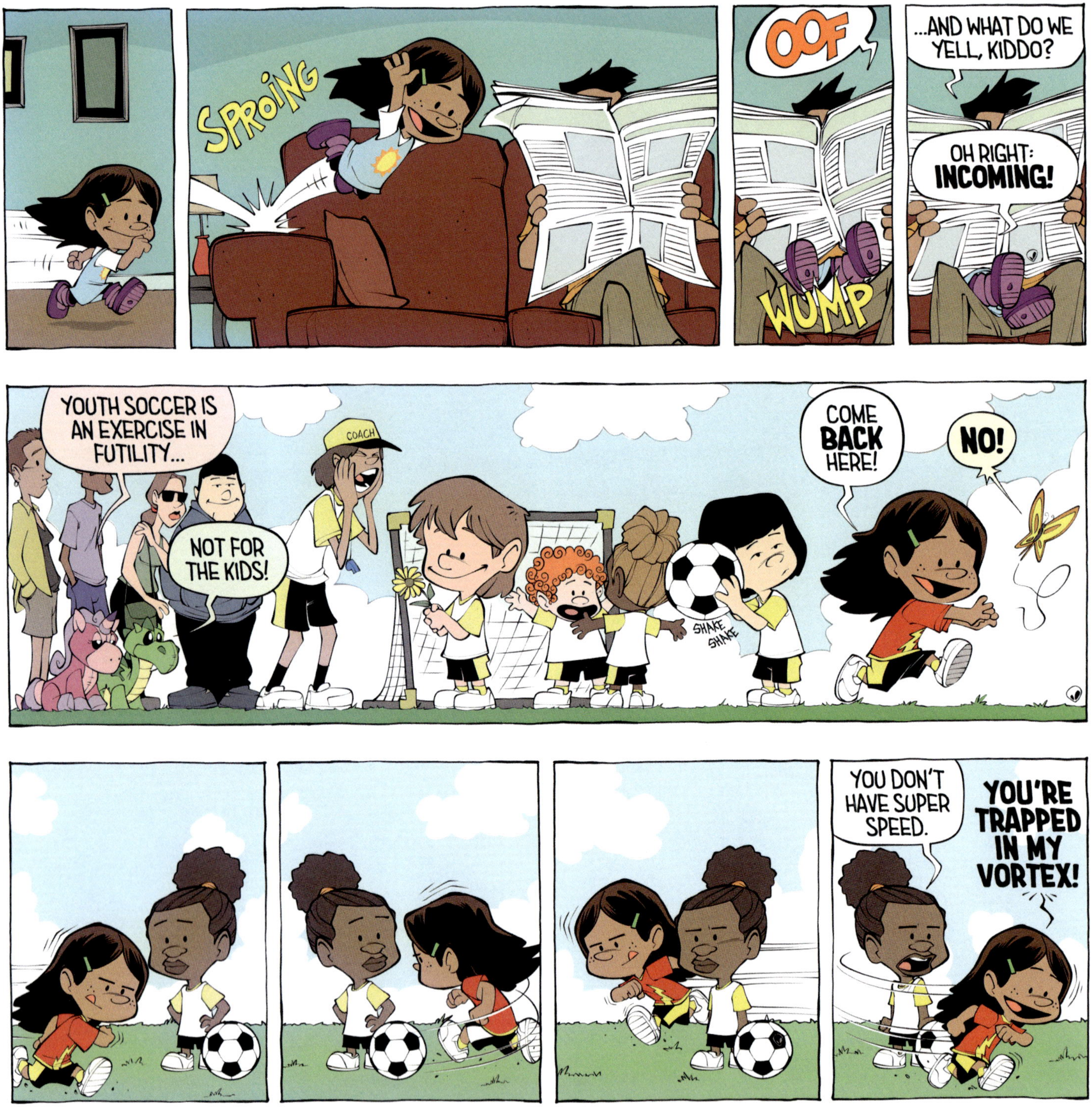
SPROING
OOF
...AND WHAT DO WE YELL, KIDDO?
OH RIGHT: INCOMING!
WUMP
YOUTH SOCCER IS AN EXERCISE IN FUTILITY...
NOT FOR THE KIDS!
COACH
SHAKE SHAKE
COME BACK HERE!
NO!
YOU DON'T HAVE SUPER SPEED.
YOU'RE TRAPPED IN MY VORTEX!

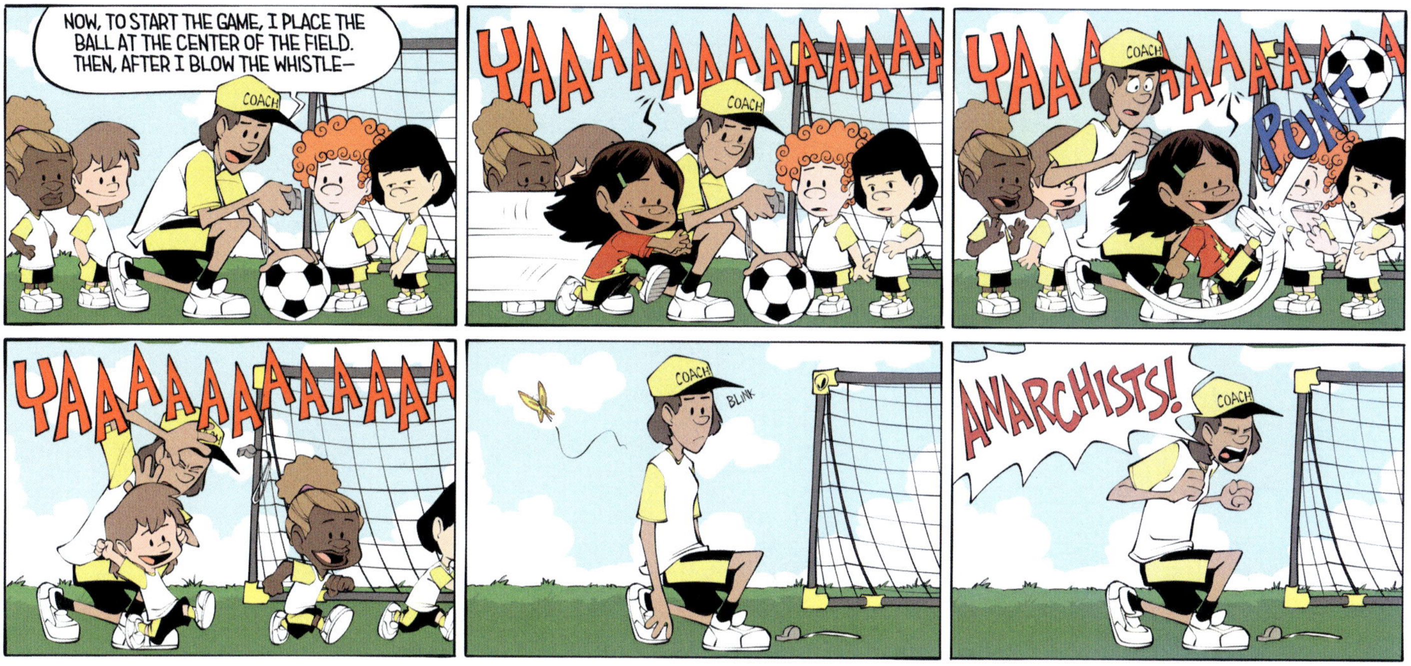
NOW, TO START THE GAME, I PLACE THE BALL AT THE CENTER OF THE FIELD. THEN, AFTER I BLOW THE WHISTLE—
COACH
YAAAAAAAAAAAA
COACH
YAAAAAAAAAA
COACH
PUNT
YAAAAAAAAAAA
BLINK
COACH
ANARCHISTS!
COACH

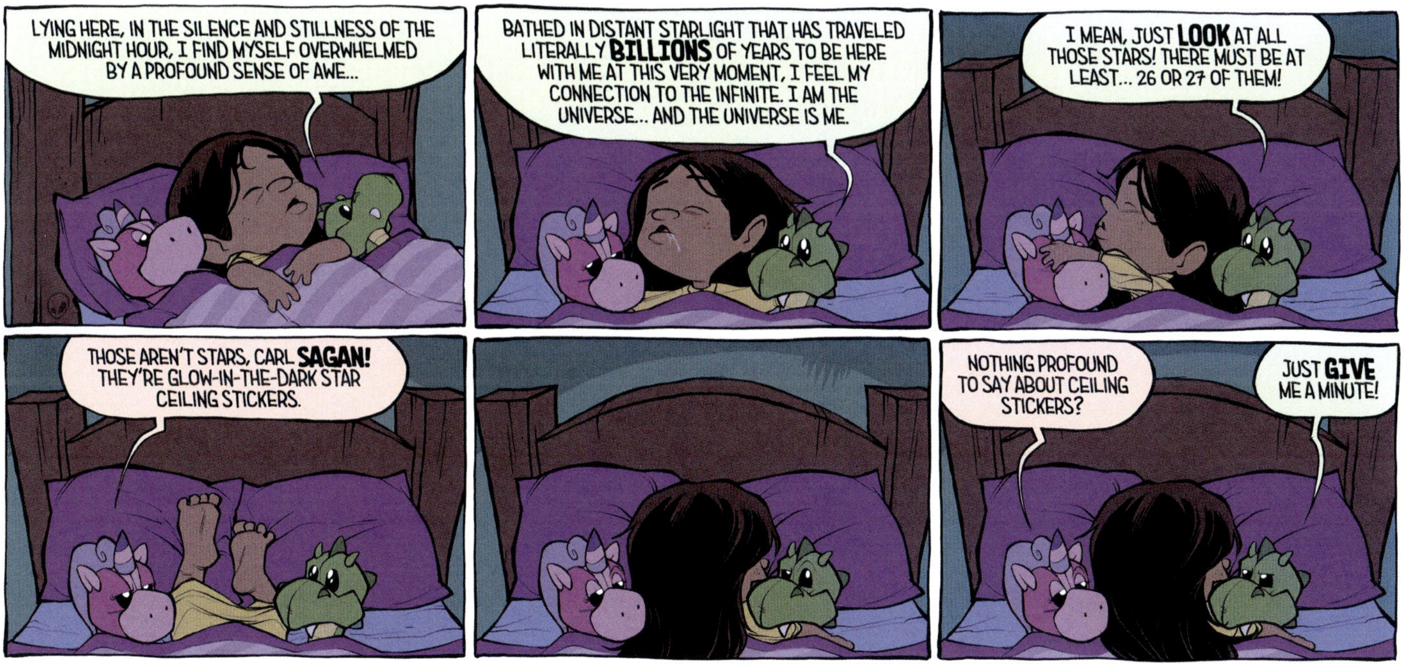
LYING HERE, IN THE SILENCE AND STILLNESS OF THE MIDNIGHT HOUR, I FIND MYSELF OVERWHELMED BY A PROFOUND SENSE OF AWE...
BATHED IN DISTANT STARLIGHT THAT HAS TRAVELED LITERALLY **BILLIONS** OF YEARS TO BE HERE WITH ME AT THIS VERY MOMENT, I FEEL MY CONNECTION TO THE INFINITE. I AM THE UNIVERSE... AND THE UNIVERSE IS ME.
I MEAN, JUST **LOOK** AT ALL THOSE STARS! THERE MUST BE AT LEAST... 26 OR 27 OF THEM!
THOSE AREN'T STARS, CARL **SAGAN!** THEY'RE GLOW-IN-THE-DARK STAR CEILING STICKERS.
NOTHING PROFOUND TO SAY ABOUT CEILING STICKERS?
JUST **GIVE** ME A MINUTE!

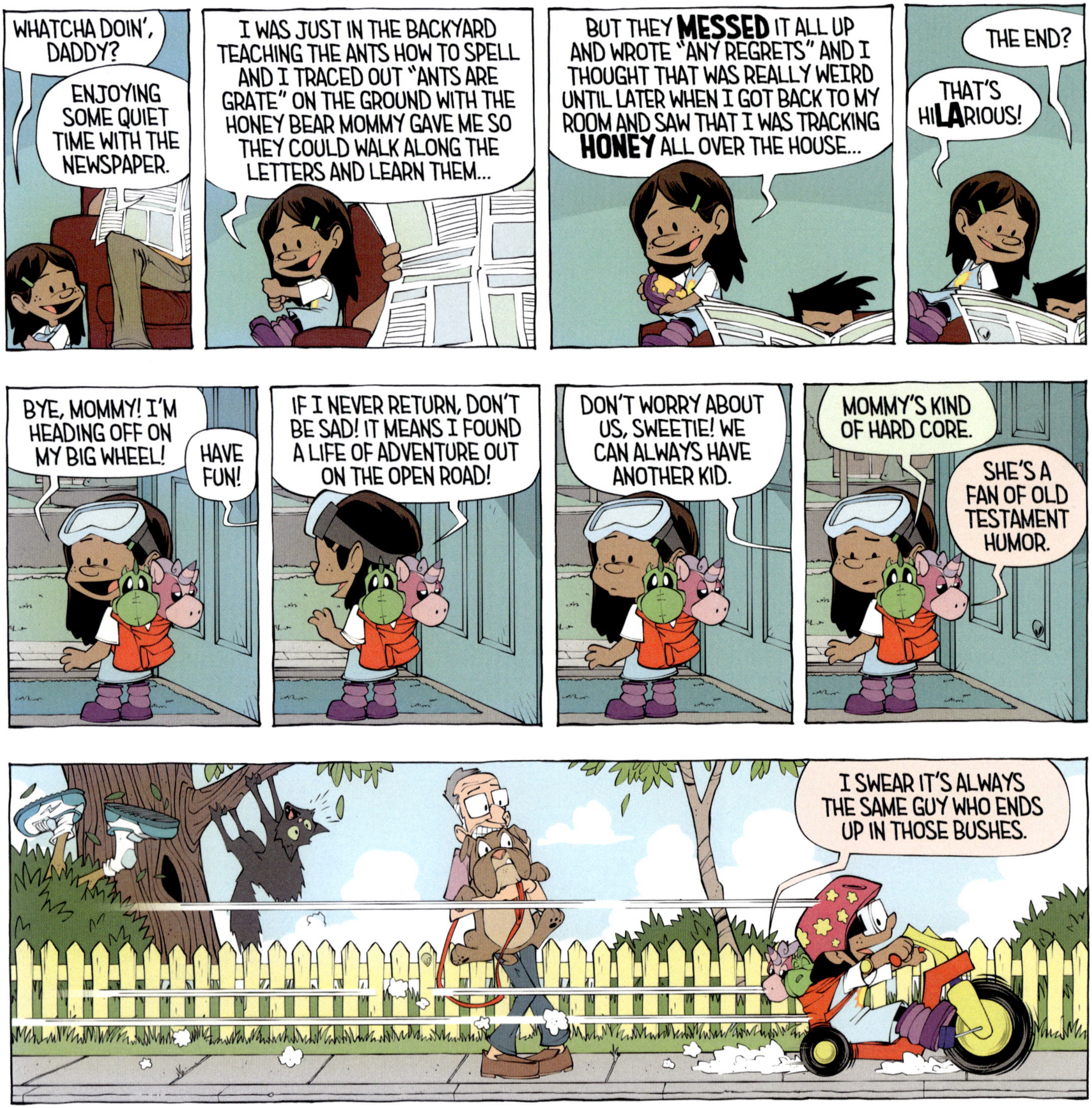
WHATCHA DOIN', DADDY?
ENJOYING SOME QUIET TIME WITH THE NEWSPAPER.
I WAS JUST IN THE BACKYARD TEACHING THE ANTS HOW TO SPELL AND I TRACED OUT "ANTS ARE GRATE" ON THE GROUND WITH THE HONEY BEAR MOMMY GAVE ME SO THEY COULD WALK ALONG THE LETTERS AND LEARN THEM...
BUT THEY **MESSED** IT ALL UP AND WROTE "ANY REGRETS" AND I THOUGHT THAT WAS REALLY WEIRD UNTIL LATER WHEN I GOT BACK TO MY ROOM AND SAW THAT I WAS TRACKING **HONEY** ALL OVER THE HOUSE...
THE END?
THAT'S HI**LA**RIOUS!
BYE, MOMMY! I'M HEADING OFF ON MY BIG WHEEL!
HAVE FUN!
IF I NEVER RETURN, DON'T BE SAD! IT MEANS I FOUND A LIFE OF ADVENTURE OUT ON THE OPEN ROAD!
DON'T WORRY ABOUT US, SWEETIE! WE CAN ALWAYS HAVE ANOTHER KID.
MOMMY'S KIND OF HARD CORE.
SHE'S A FAN OF OLD TESTAMENT HUMOR.
I SWEAR IT'S ALWAYS THE SAME GUY WHO ENDS UP IN THOSE BUSHES.

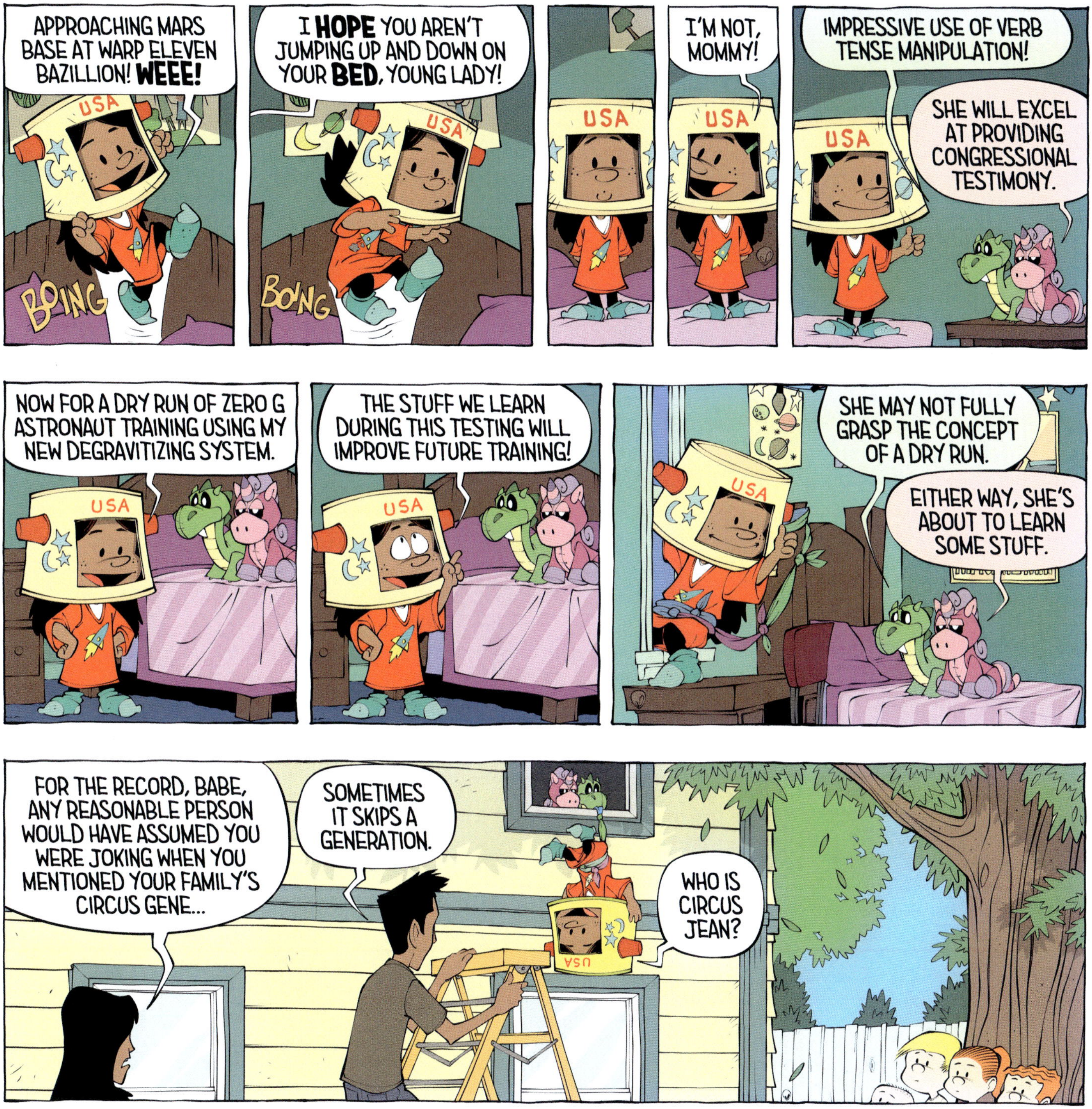

APPROACHING MARS BASE AT WARP ELEVEN BAZILLION! **WEEE!**
BOING
I **HOPE** YOU AREN'T JUMPING UP AND DOWN ON YOUR **BED**, YOUNG LADY!
BOING
I'M NOT, MOMMY!
IMPRESSIVE USE OF VERB TENSE MANIPULATION!
SHE WILL EXCEL AT PROVIDING CONGRESSIONAL TESTIMONY.
NOW FOR A DRY RUN OF ZERO G ASTRONAUT TRAINING USING MY NEW DEGRAVITIZING SYSTEM.
THE STUFF WE LEARN DURING THIS TESTING WILL IMPROVE FUTURE TRAINING!
SHE MAY NOT FULLY GRASP THE CONCEPT OF A DRY RUN.
EITHER WAY, SHE'S ABOUT TO LEARN SOME STUFF.
FOR THE RECORD, BABE, ANY REASONABLE PERSON WOULD HAVE ASSUMED YOU WERE JOKING WHEN YOU MENTIONED YOUR FAMILY'S CIRCUS GENE...
SOMETIMES IT SKIPS A GENERATION.
WHO IS CIRCUS JEAN?

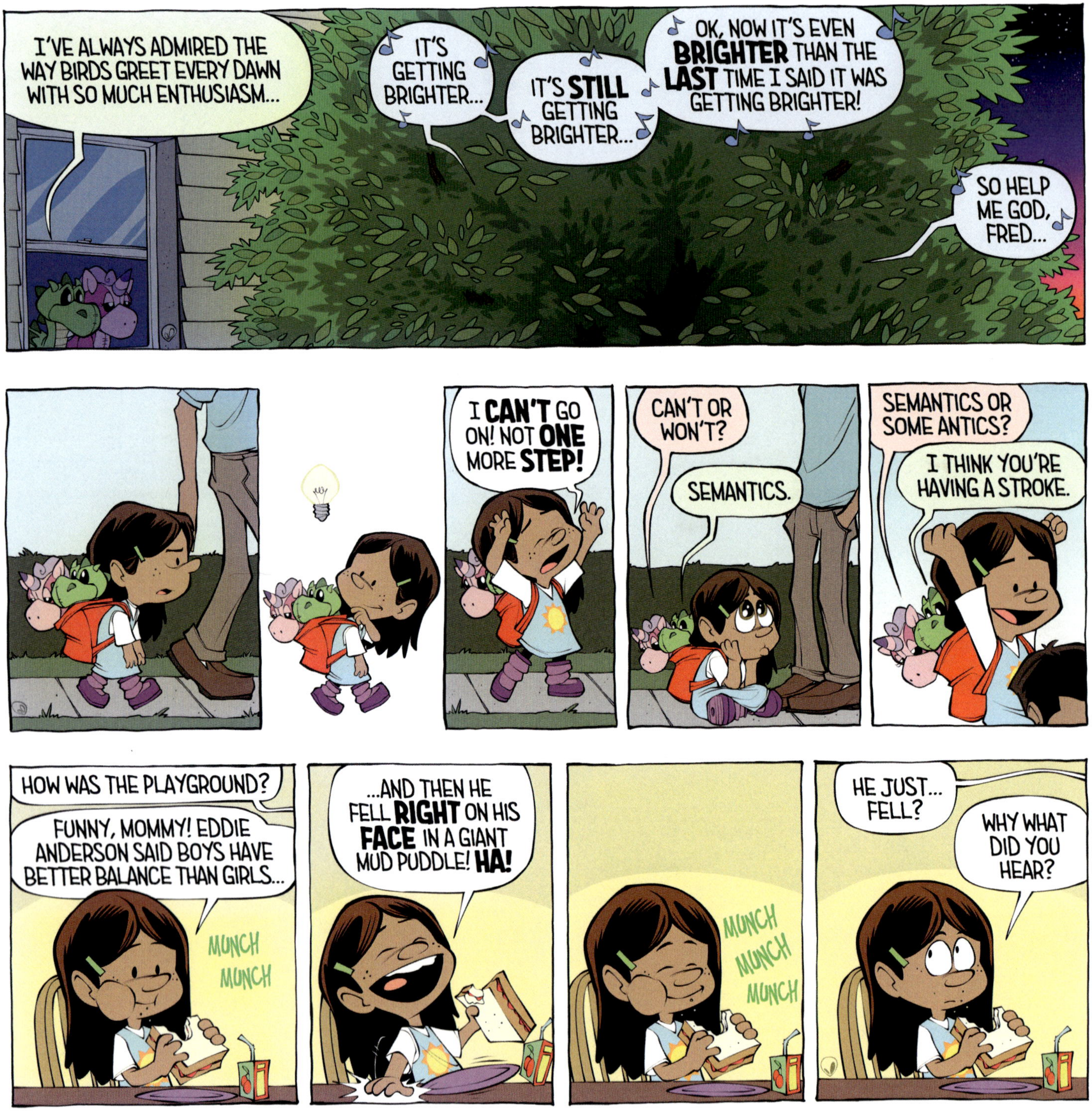
I'VE ALWAYS ADMIRED THE WAY BIRDS GREET EVERY DAWN WITH SO MUCH ENTHUSIASM...
IT'S GETTING BRIGHTER...
IT'S STILL GETTING BRIGHTER...
OK, NOW IT'S EVEN BRIGHTER THAN THE LAST TIME I SAID IT WAS GETTING BRIGHTER!
SO HELP ME GOD, FRED...
I CAN'T GO ON! NOT ONE MORE STEP!
CAN'T OR WON'T?
SEMANTICS.
SEMANTICS OR SOME ANTICS?
I THINK YOU'RE HAVING A STROKE.
HOW WAS THE PLAYGROUND?
FUNNY, MOMMY! EDDIE ANDERSON SAID BOYS HAVE BETTER BALANCE THAN GIRLS...
MUNCH
MUNCH
...AND THEN HE FELL RIGHT ON HIS FACE IN A GIANT MUD PUDDLE! HA!
MUNCH
MUNCH
MUNCH
HE JUST... FELL?
WHY WHAT DID YOU HEAR?

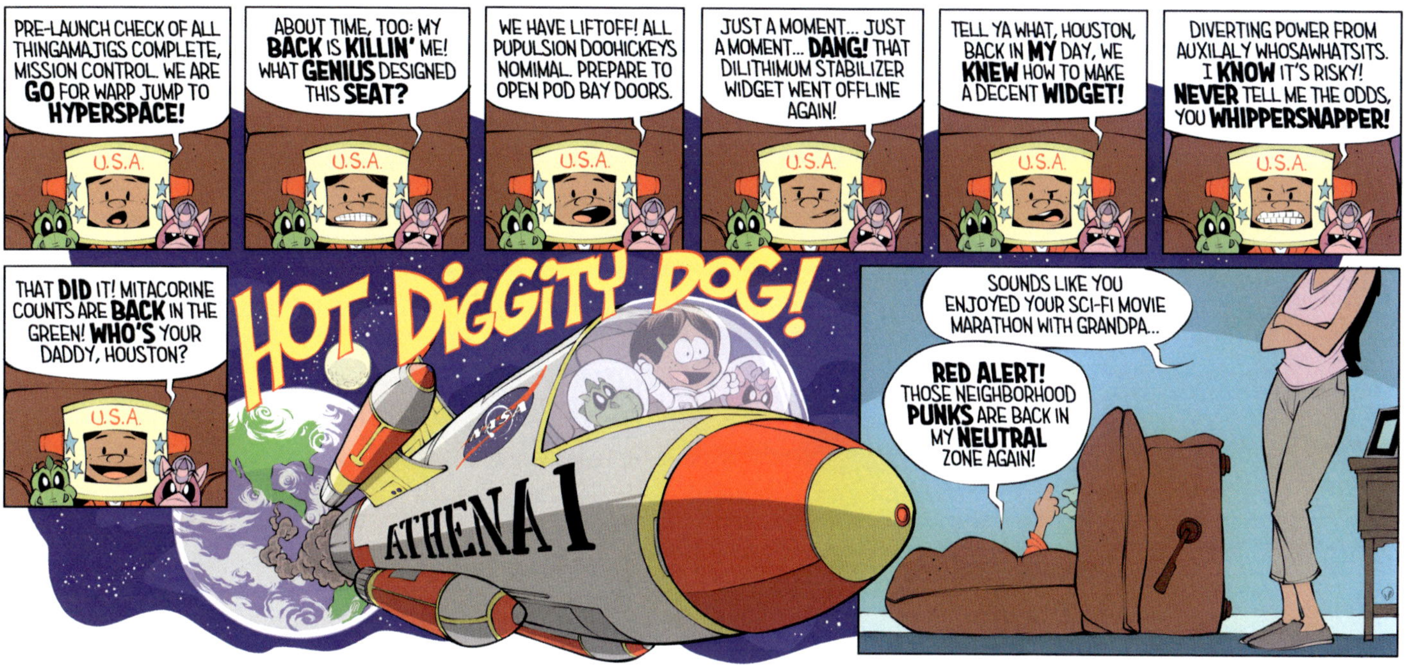
PRE-LAUNCH CHECK OF ALL THINGAMAJIGS COMPLETE, MISSION CONTROL. WE ARE GO FOR WARP JUMP TO HYPERSPACE!
U.S.A.
ABOUT TIME, TOO: MY BACK IS KILLIN' ME! WHAT GENIUS DESIGNED THIS SEAT?
WE HAVE LIFTOFF! ALL PUPULSION DOOHICKEYS NOMIMAL. PREPARE TO OPEN POD BAY DOORS.
JUST A MOMENT... JUST A MOMENT... DANG! THAT DILITHIMUM STABILIZER WIDGET WENT OFFLINE AGAIN!
TELL YA WHAT, HOUSTON, BACK IN MY DAY, WE KNEW HOW TO MAKE A DECENT WIDGET!
DIVERTING POWER FROM AUXILALY WHOSAWHATSITS. I KNOW IT'S RISKY! NEVER TELL ME THE ODDS, YOU WHIPPERSNAPPER!
THAT DID IT! MITACORINE COUNTS ARE BACK IN THE GREEN! WHO'S YOUR DADDY, HOUSTON?
HOT DIGGITY DOG!
ATHENA 1
SOUNDS LIKE YOU ENJOYED YOUR SCI-FI MOVIE MARATHON WITH GRANDPA...
RED ALERT! THOSE NEIGHBORHOOD PUNKS ARE BACK IN MY NEUTRAL ZONE AGAIN!

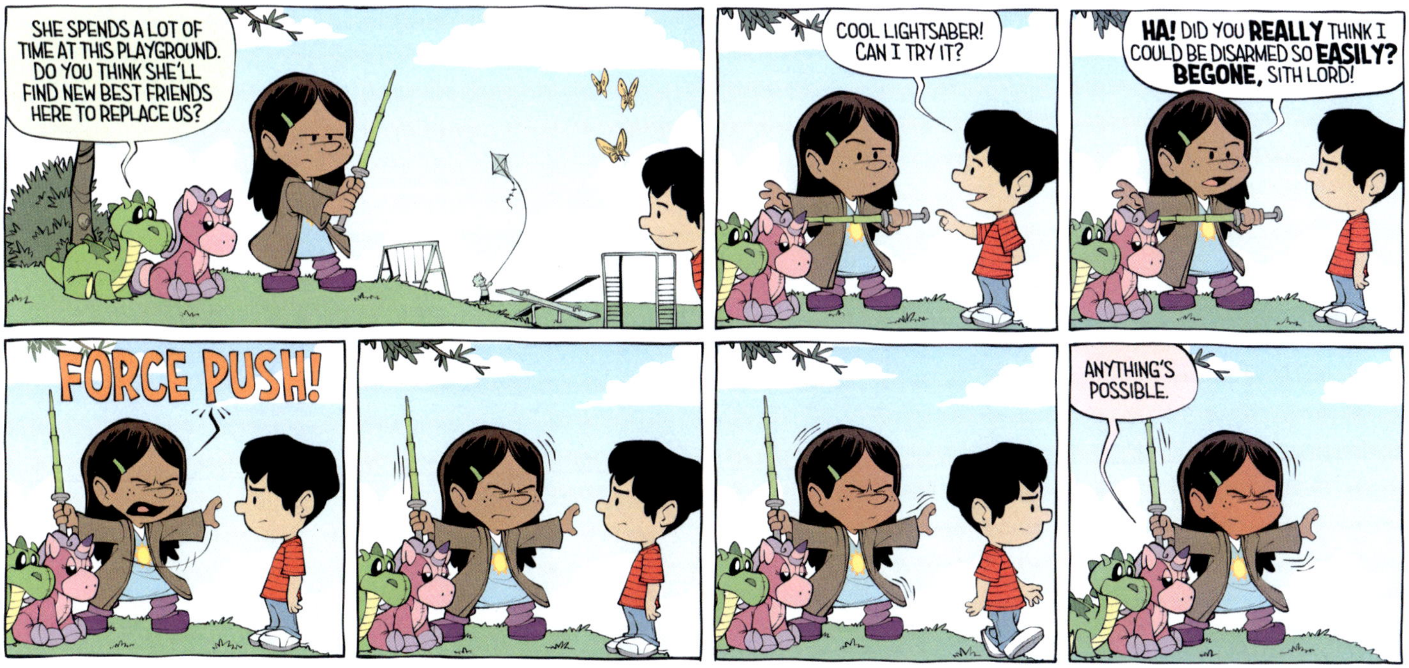
SHE SPENDS A LOT OF TIME AT THIS PLAYGROUND. DO YOU THINK SHE'LL FIND NEW BEST FRIENDS HERE TO REPLACE US?
COOL LIGHTSABER! CAN I TRY IT?
HA! DID YOU REALLY THINK I COULD BE DISARMED SO EASILY? BEGONE, SITH LORD!
FORCE PUSH!
ANYTHING'S POSSIBLE.

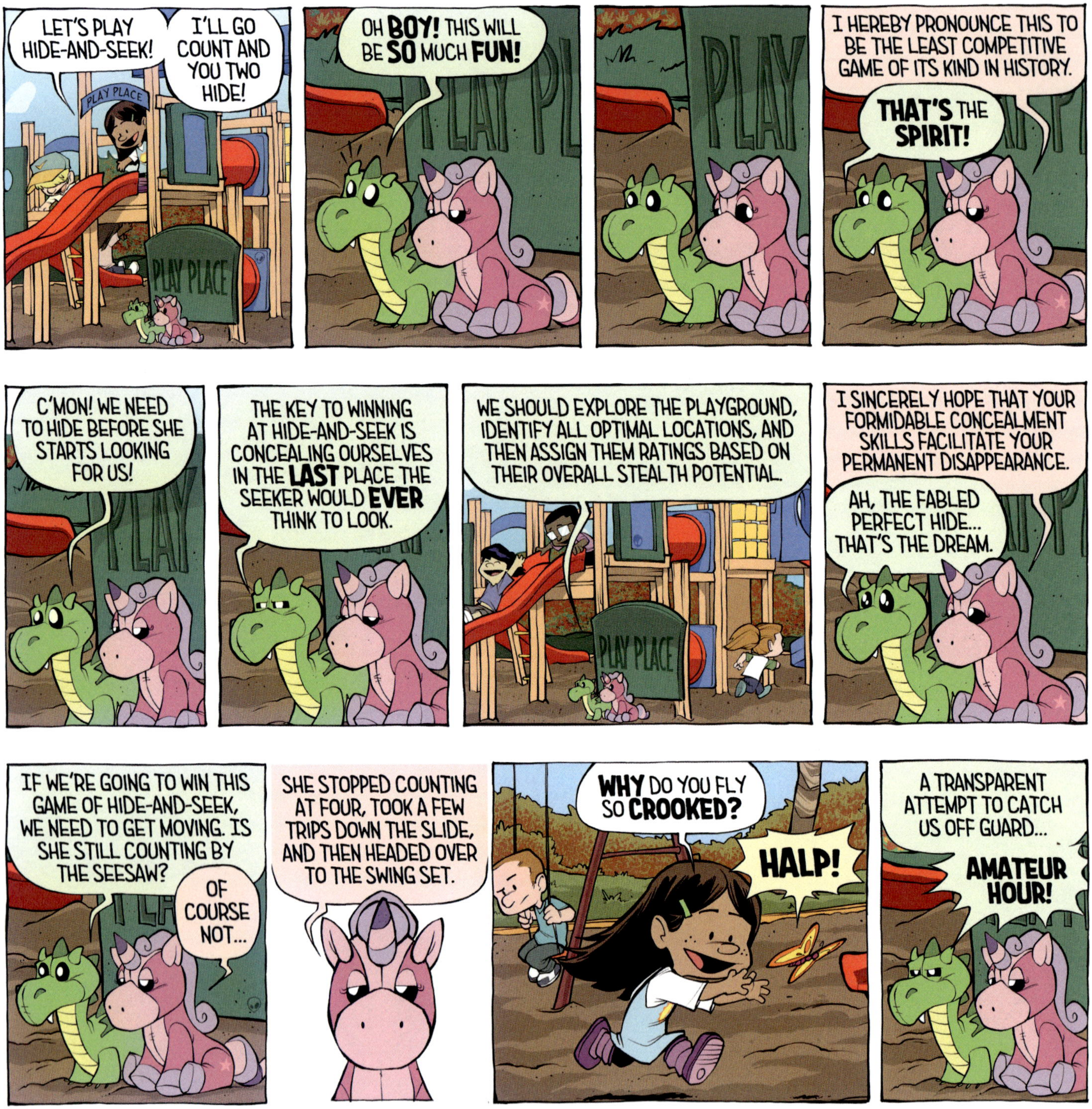
LET'S PLAY HIDE-AND-SEEK!
I'LL GO COUNT AND YOU TWO HIDE!
PLAY PLACE
PLAY PLACE
OH BOY! THIS WILL BE SO MUCH FUN!
PLAY
I HEREBY PRONOUNCE THIS TO BE THE LEAST COMPETITIVE GAME OF ITS KIND IN HISTORY.
THAT'S THE SPIRIT!
C'MON! WE NEED TO HIDE BEFORE SHE STARTS LOOKING FOR US!
THE KEY TO WINNING AT HIDE-AND-SEEK IS CONCEALING OURSELVES IN THE LAST PLACE THE SEEKER WOULD EVER THINK TO LOOK.
WE SHOULD EXPLORE THE PLAYGROUND, IDENTIFY ALL OPTIMAL LOCATIONS, AND THEN ASSIGN THEM RATINGS BASED ON THEIR OVERALL STEALTH POTENTIAL.
PLAY PLACE
I SINCERELY HOPE THAT YOUR FORMIDABLE CONCEALMENT SKILLS FACILITATE YOUR PERMANENT DISAPPEARANCE.
AH, THE FABLED PERFECT HIDE... THAT'S THE DREAM.
IF WE'RE GOING TO WIN THIS GAME OF HIDE-AND-SEEK, WE NEED TO GET MOVING. IS SHE STILL COUNTING BY THE SEESAW?
OF COURSE NOT...
SHE STOPPED COUNTING AT FOUR, TOOK A FEW TRIPS DOWN THE SLIDE, AND THEN HEADED OVER TO THE SWING SET.
WHY DO YOU FLY SO CROOKED?
HALP!
A TRANSPARENT ATTEMPT TO CATCH US OFF GUARD...
AMATEUR HOUR!

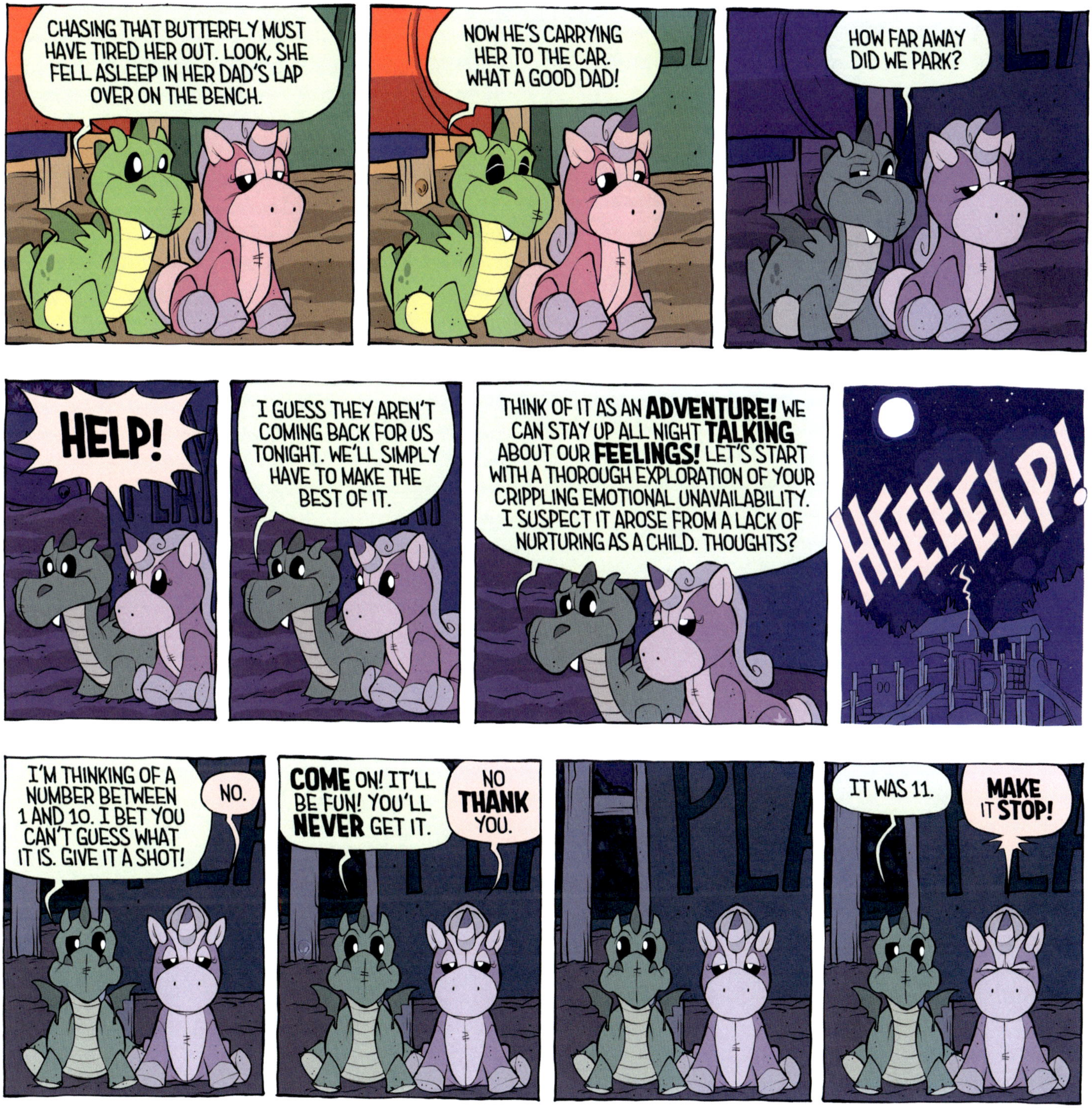
CHASING THAT BUTTERFLY MUST HAVE TIRED HER OUT. LOOK, SHE FELL ASLEEP IN HER DAD'S LAP OVER ON THE BENCH.
NOW HE'S CARRYING HER TO THE CAR. WHAT A GOOD DAD!
HOW FAR AWAY DID WE PARK?
HELP!
I GUESS THEY AREN'T COMING BACK FOR US TONIGHT. WE'LL SIMPLY HAVE TO MAKE THE BEST OF IT.
THINK OF IT AS AN ADVENTURE! WE CAN STAY UP ALL NIGHT TALKING ABOUT OUR FEELINGS! LET'S START WITH A THOROUGH EXPLORATION OF YOUR CRIPPLING EMOTIONAL UNAVAILABILITY. I SUSPECT IT AROSE FROM A LACK OF NURTURING AS A CHILD. THOUGHTS?
HEEEELP!
I'M THINKING OF A NUMBER BETWEEN 1 AND 10. I BET YOU CAN'T GUESS WHAT IT IS. GIVE IT A SHOT!
NO.
COME ON! IT'LL BE FUN! YOU'LL NEVER GET IT.
NO THANK YOU.
IT WAS 11.
MAKE IT STOP!

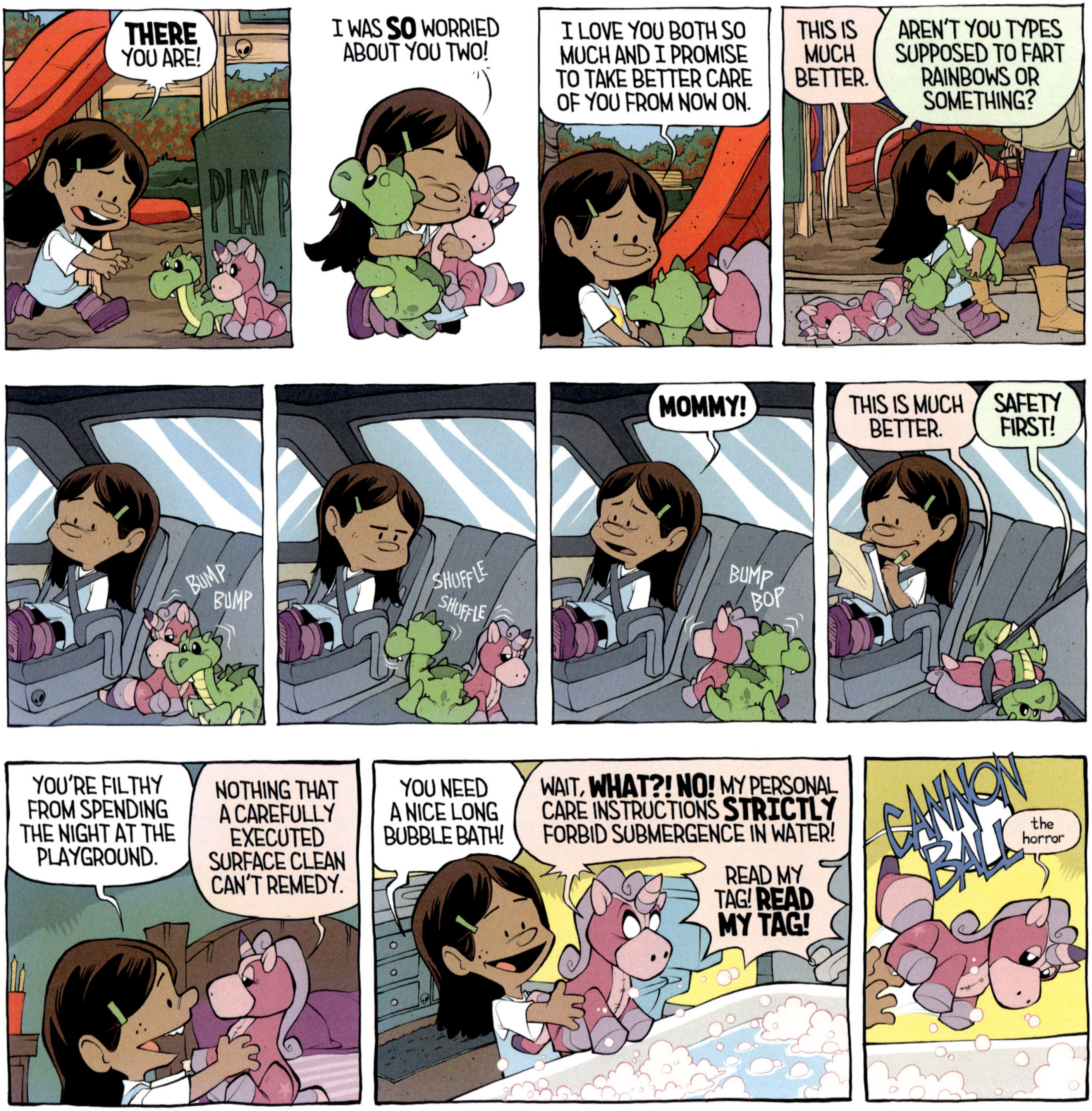
THERE YOU ARE!
PLAY P
I WAS SO WORRIED ABOUT YOU TWO!
I LOVE YOU BOTH SO MUCH AND I PROMISE TO TAKE BETTER CARE OF YOU FROM NOW ON.
THIS IS MUCH BETTER.
AREN'T YOU TYPES SUPPOSED TO FART RAINBOWS OR SOMETHING?
BUMP BUMP
SHUFFLE SHUFFLE
MOMMY!
BUMP BOP
THIS IS MUCH BETTER.
SAFETY FIRST!
YOU'RE FILTHY FROM SPENDING THE NIGHT AT THE PLAYGROUND.
NOTHING THAT A CAREFULLY EXECUTED SURFACE CLEAN CAN'T REMEDY.
YOU NEED A NICE LONG BUBBLE BATH!
WAIT, WHAT?! NO! MY PERSONAL CARE INSTRUCTIONS STRICTLY FORBID SUBMERGENCE IN WATER!
READ MY TAG! READ MY TAG!
CANNON BALL
the horror

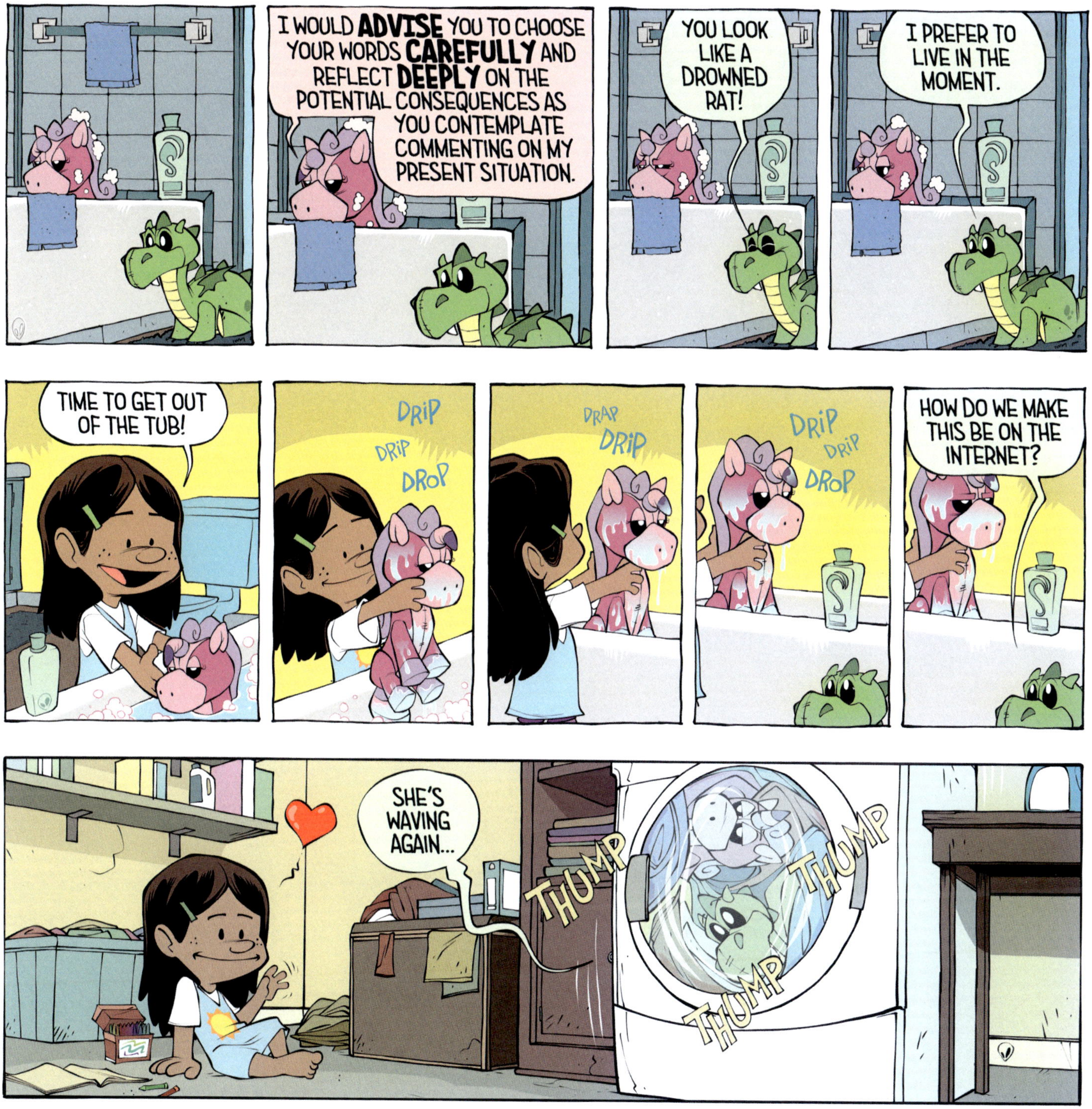

I WOULD **ADVISE** YOU TO CHOOSE YOUR WORDS **CAREFULLY** AND REFLECT **DEEPLY** ON THE POTENTIAL CONSEQUENCES AS YOU CONTEMPLATE COMMENTING ON MY PRESENT SITUATION.
YOU LOOK LIKE A DROWNED RAT!
I PREFER TO LIVE IN THE MOMENT.
TIME TO GET OUT OF THE TUB!
DRIP
DRIP
DROP
DRAP
DRIP
DRIP
DRIP
DROP
HOW DO WE MAKE THIS BE ON THE INTERNET?
SHE'S WAVING AGAIN...
THUMP
THUMP
THUMP
THUMP

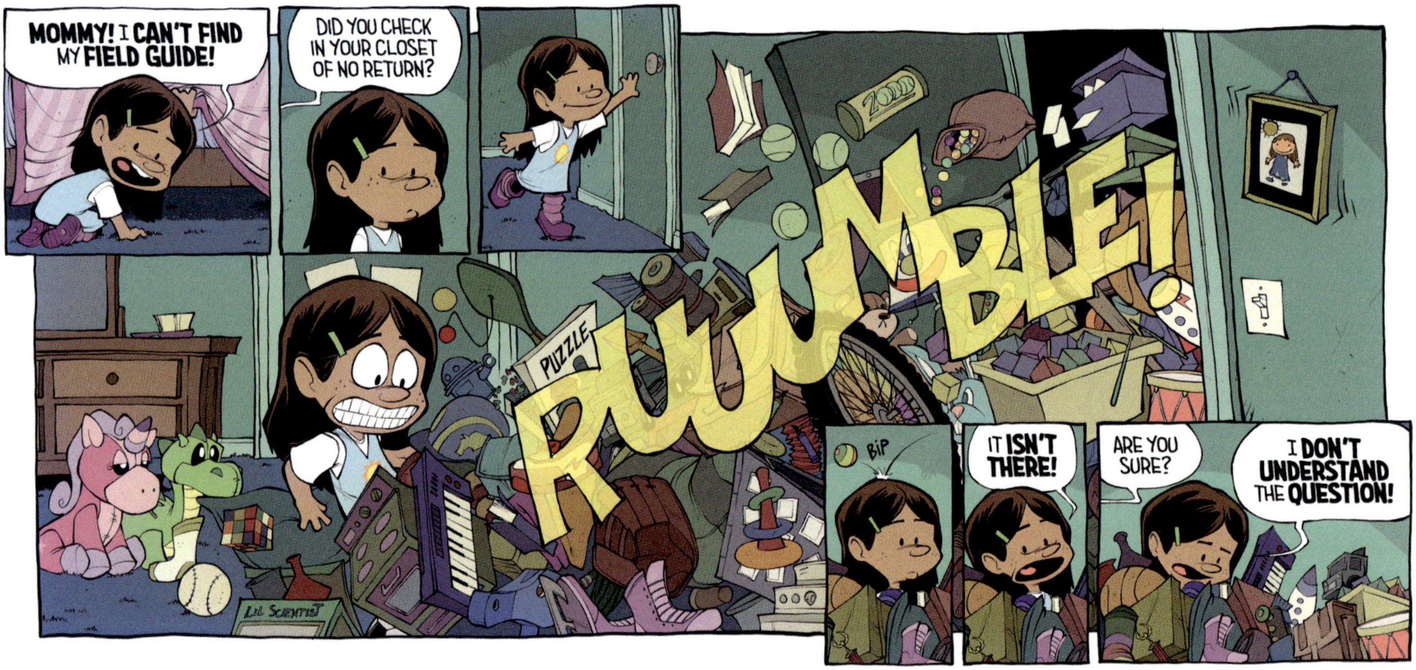
MOMMY! I CAN'T FIND MY FIELD GUIDE!
DID YOU CHECK IN YOUR CLOSET OF NO RETURN?
RUUMBLE!
PUZZLE
LIL SCIENTIST
BIP
IT ISN'T THERE!
ARE YOU SURE?
I DON'T UNDERSTAND THE QUESTION!

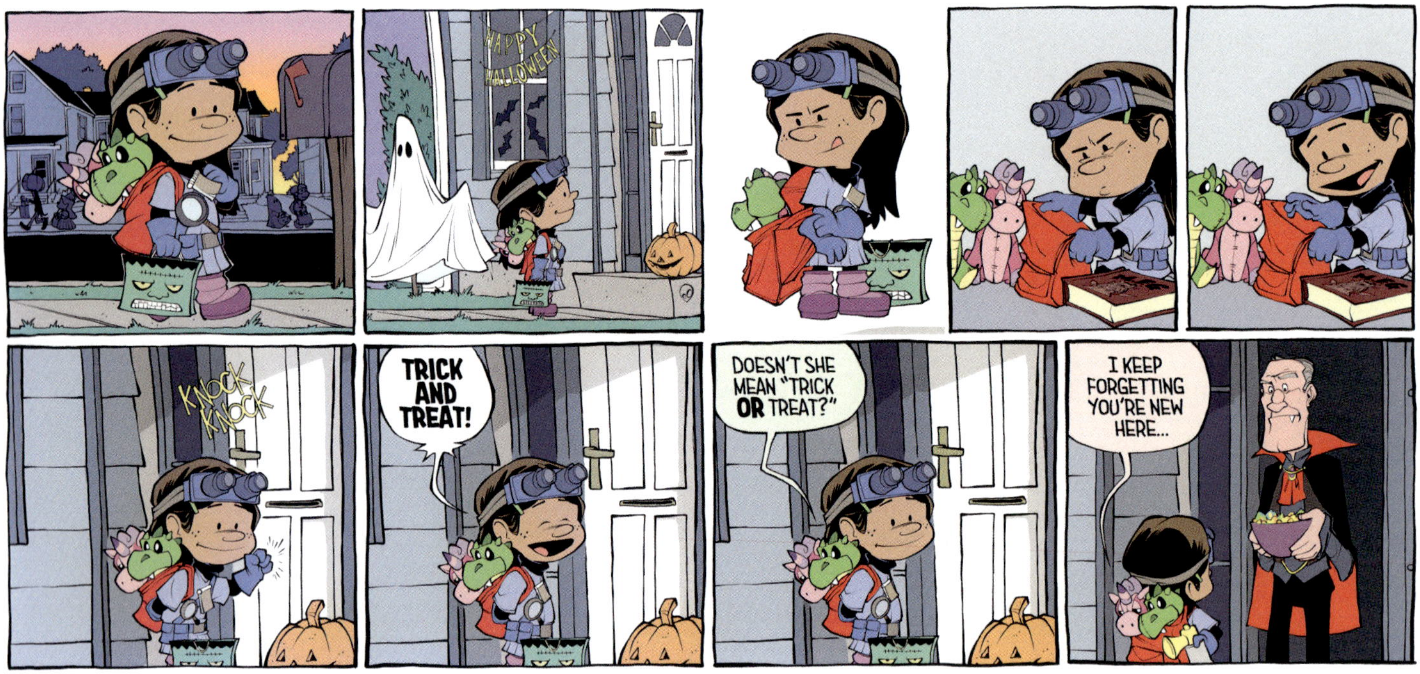
HAPPY HALLOWEEN
KNOCK KNOCK
TRICK AND TREAT!
DOESN'T SHE MEAN "TRICK OR TREAT?"
I KEEP FORGETTING YOU'RE NEW HERE...

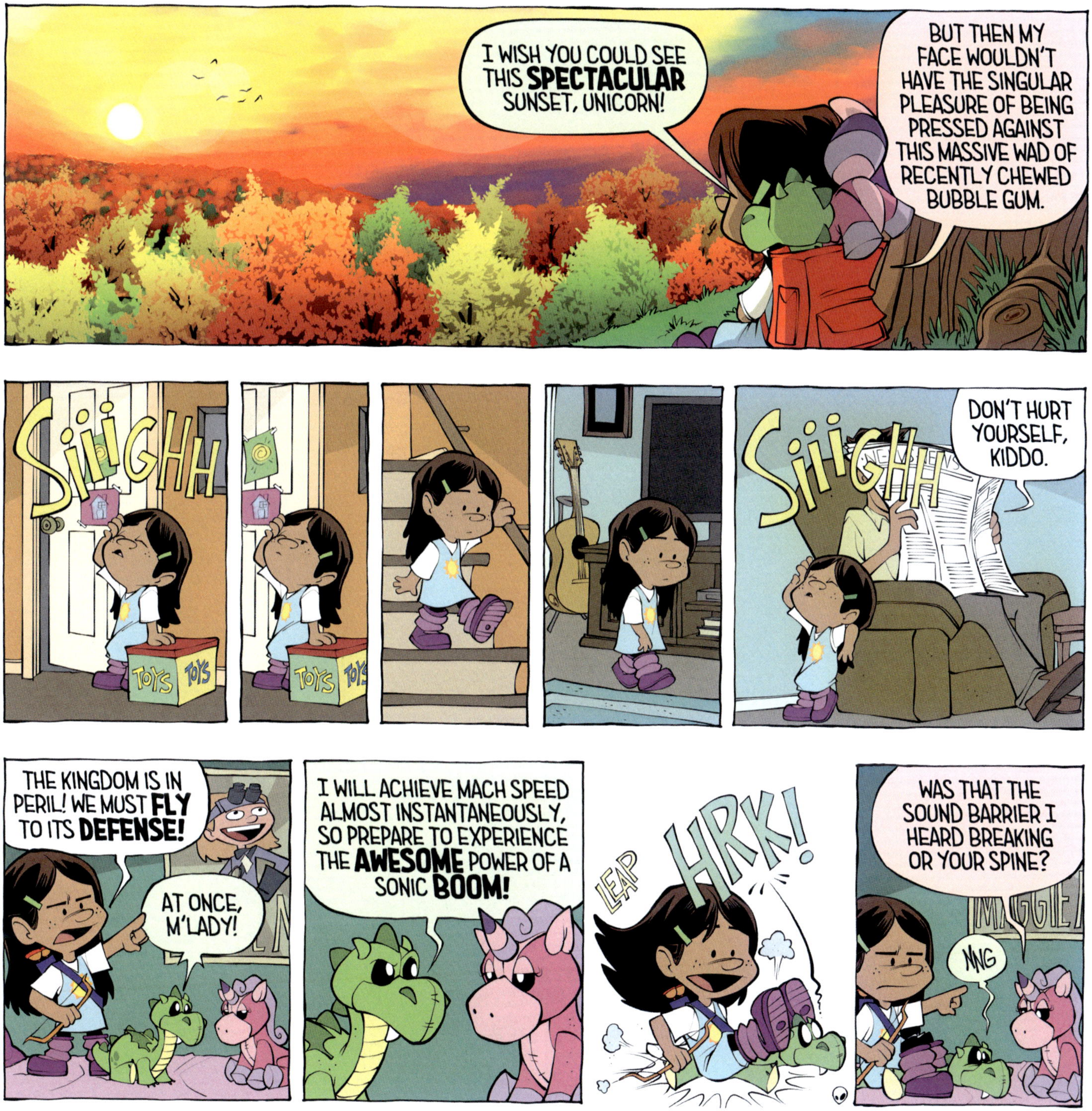

I WISH YOU COULD SEE THIS SPECTACULAR SUNSET, UNICORN!
BUT THEN MY FACE WOULDN'T HAVE THE SINGULAR PLEASURE OF BEING PRESSED AGAINST THIS MASSIVE WAD OF RECENTLY CHEWED BUBBLE GUM.
SIIIGHH
TOYS
TOYS
SIIIGHH
DON'T HURT YOURSELF, KIDDO.
THE KINGDOM IS IN PERIL! WE MUST FLY TO ITS DEFENSE!
AT ONCE, M'LADY!
I WILL ACHIEVE MACH SPEED ALMOST INSTANTANEOUSLY, SO PREPARE TO EXPERIENCE THE AWESOME POWER OF A SONIC BOOM!
LEAP
HRK!
WAS THAT THE SOUND BARRIER I HEARD BREAKING OR YOUR SPINE?
NNG

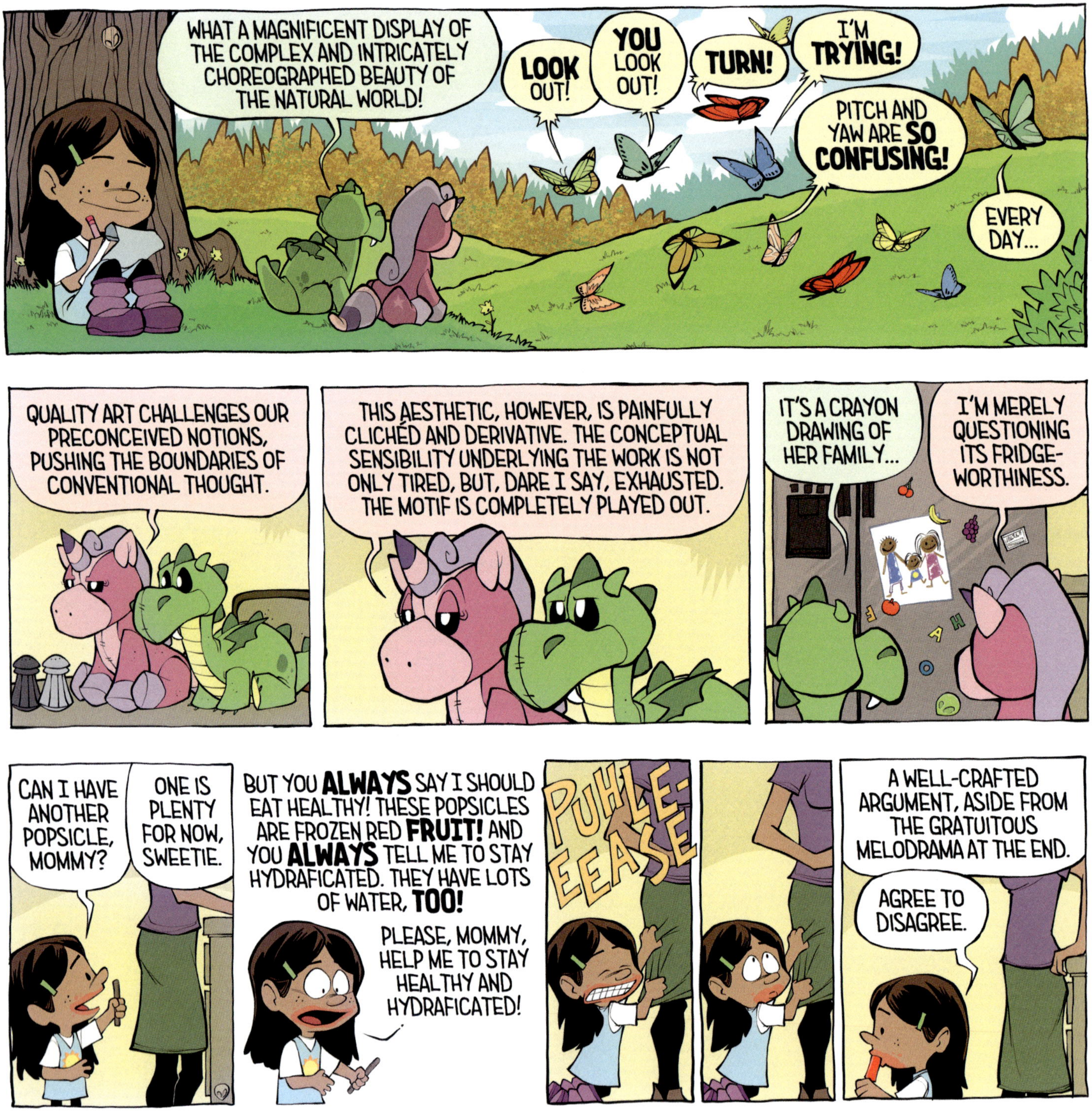

WHAT A MAGNIFICENT DISPLAY OF THE COMPLEX AND INTRICATELY CHOREOGRAPHED BEAUTY OF THE NATURAL WORLD!
LOOK OUT!
YOU LOOK OUT!
TURN!
I'M TRYING!
PITCH AND YAW ARE SO CONFUSING!
EVERY DAY...
QUALITY ART CHALLENGES OUR PRECONCEIVED NOTIONS, PUSHING THE BOUNDARIES OF CONVENTIONAL THOUGHT.
THIS AESTHETIC, HOWEVER, IS PAINFULLY CLICHÉD AND DERIVATIVE. THE CONCEPTUAL SENSIBILITY UNDERLYING THE WORK IS NOT ONLY TIRED, BUT, DARE I SAY, EXHAUSTED. THE MOTIF IS COMPLETELY PLAYED OUT.
IT'S A CRAYON DRAWING OF HER FAMILY...
I'M MERELY QUESTIONING ITS FRIDGE-WORTHINESS.
CAN I HAVE ANOTHER POPSICLE, MOMMY?
ONE IS PLENTY FOR NOW, SWEETIE.
BUT YOU ALWAYS SAY I SHOULD EAT HEALTHY! THESE POPSICLES ARE FROZEN RED FRUIT! AND YOU ALWAYS TELL ME TO STAY HYDRAFICATED. THEY HAVE LOTS OF WATER, TOO!
PLEASE, MOMMY, HELP ME TO STAY HEALTHY AND HYDRAFICATED!
PUHLE-EEASE
A WELL-CRAFTED ARGUMENT, ASIDE FROM THE GRATUITOUS MELODRAMA AT THE END.
AGREE TO DISAGREE.

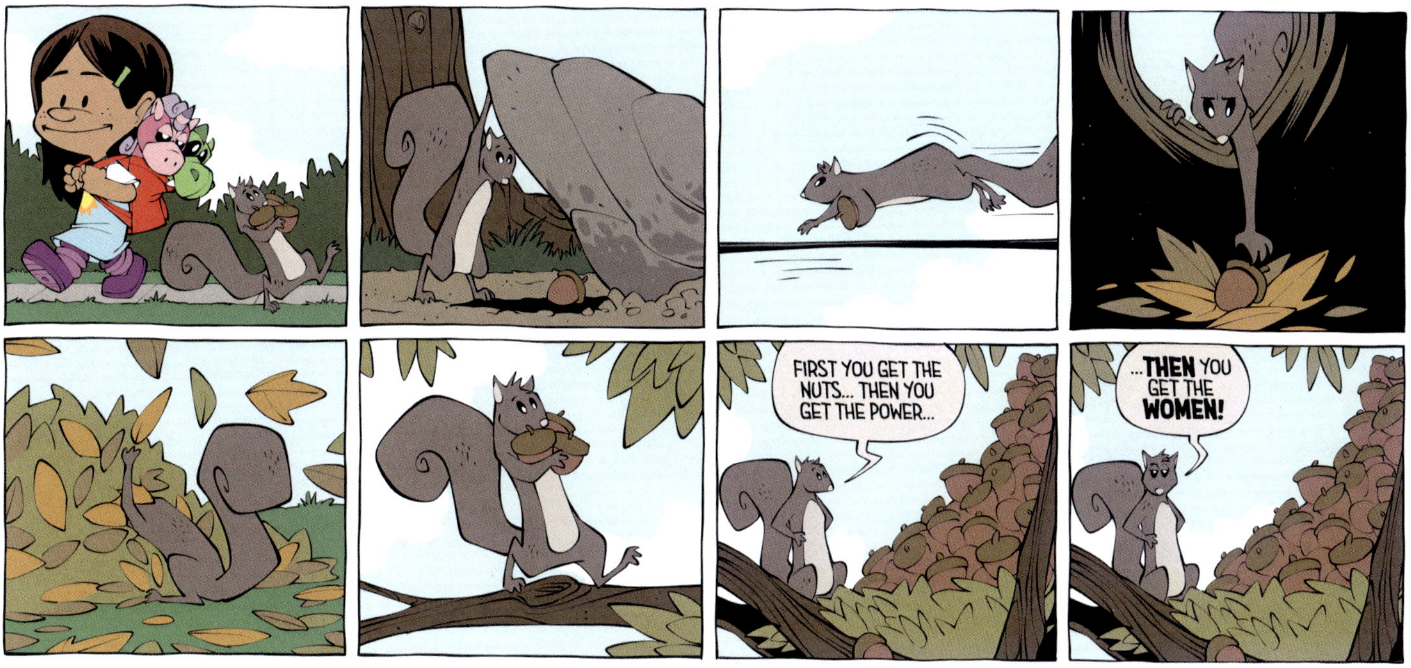
FIRST YOU GET THE NUTS... THEN YOU GET THE POWER...
...THEN YOU GET THE WOMEN!

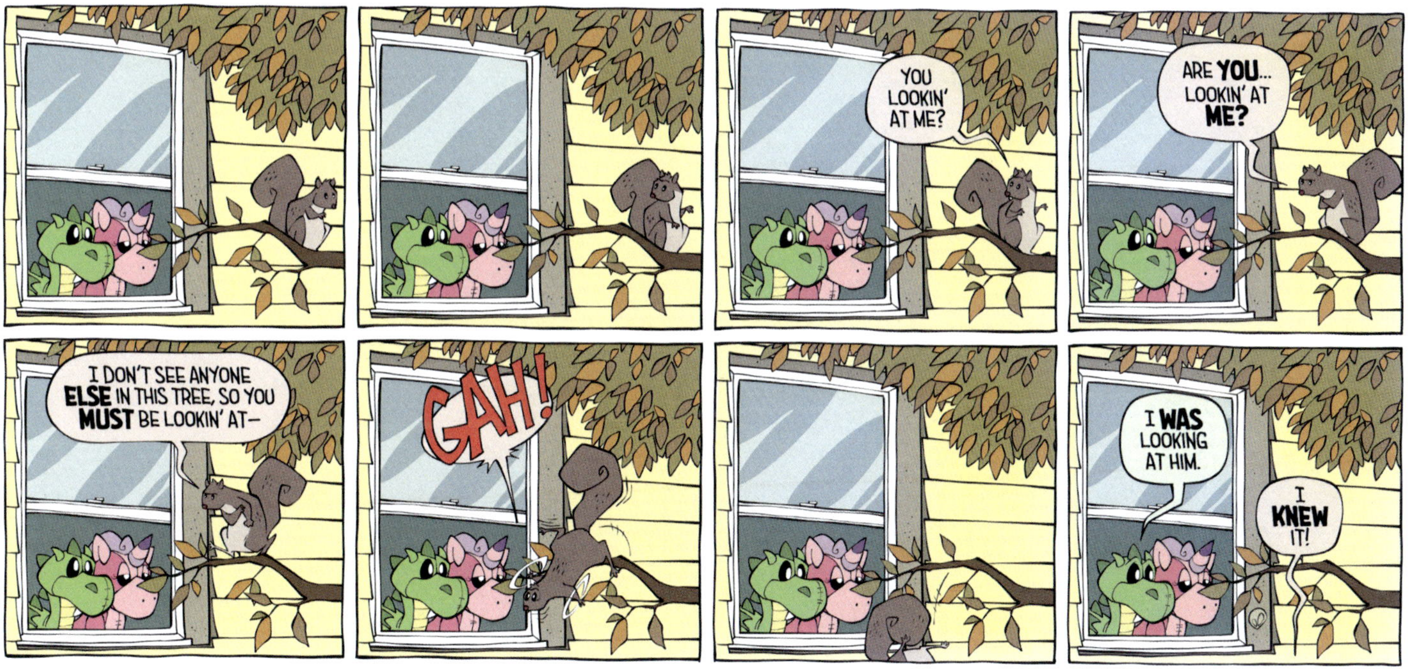
YOU LOOKIN' AT ME?
ARE YOU... LOOKIN' AT ME?
I DON'T SEE ANYONE ELSE IN THIS TREE, SO YOU MUST BE LOOKIN' AT—
GAH!
I WAS LOOKING AT HIM.
I KNEW IT!

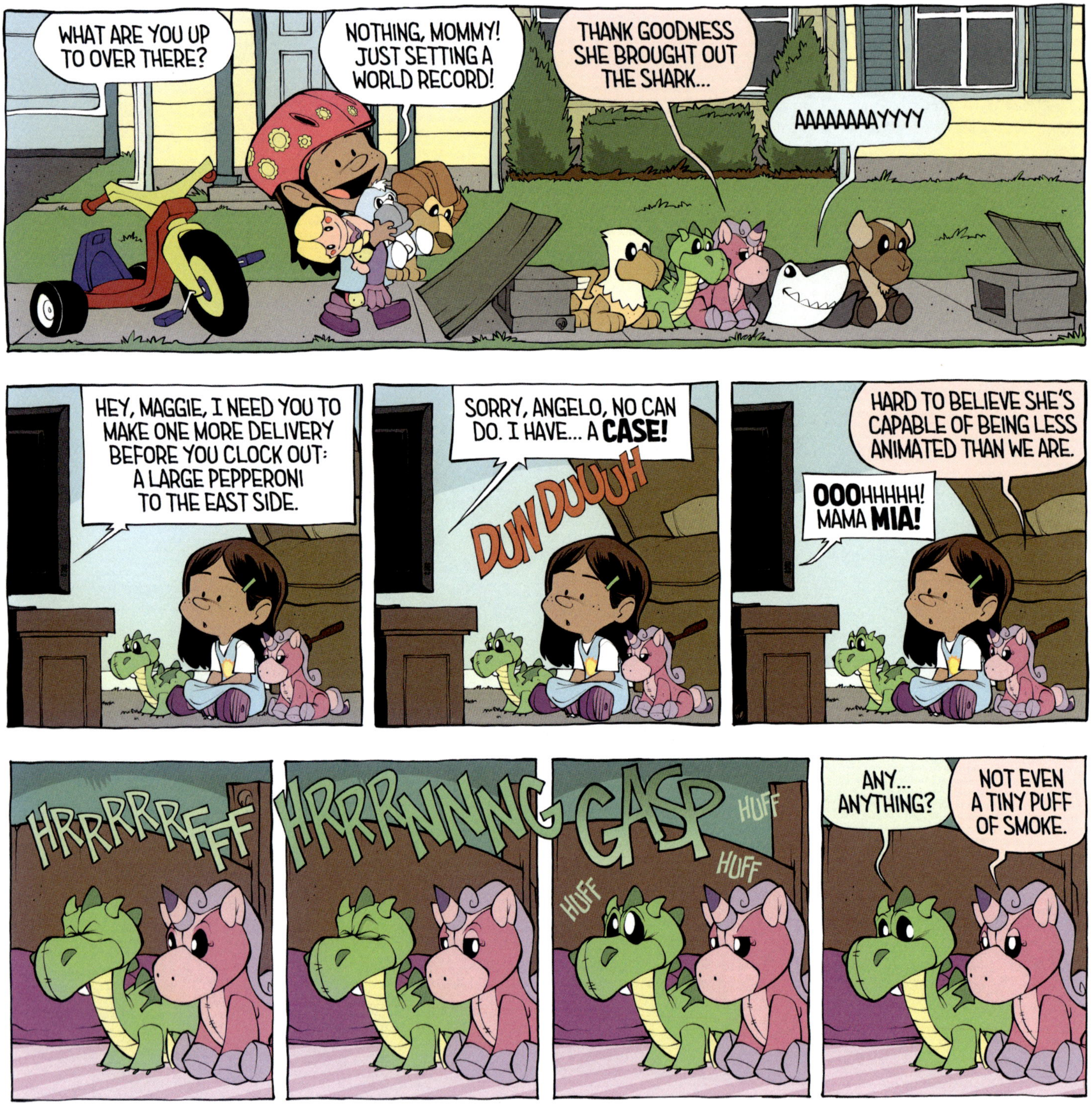
WHAT ARE YOU UP TO OVER THERE?
NOTHING, MOMMY! JUST SETTING A WORLD RECORD!
THANK GOODNESS SHE BROUGHT OUT THE SHARK...
AAAAAAAAYYYY
HEY, MAGGIE, I NEED YOU TO MAKE ONE MORE DELIVERY BEFORE YOU CLOCK OUT: A LARGE PEPPERONI TO THE EAST SIDE.
SORRY, ANGELO, NO CAN DO. I HAVE... A **CASE!**
DUN DUUUH
HARD TO BELIEVE SHE'S CAPABLE OF BEING LESS ANIMATED THAN WE ARE.
OOOHHHHH! MAMA **MIA!**
HRRRRRRFFFF
HRRRNNNNG
GASP
HUFF
HUFF
HUFF
ANY... ANYTHING?
NOT EVEN A TINY PUFF OF SMOKE.

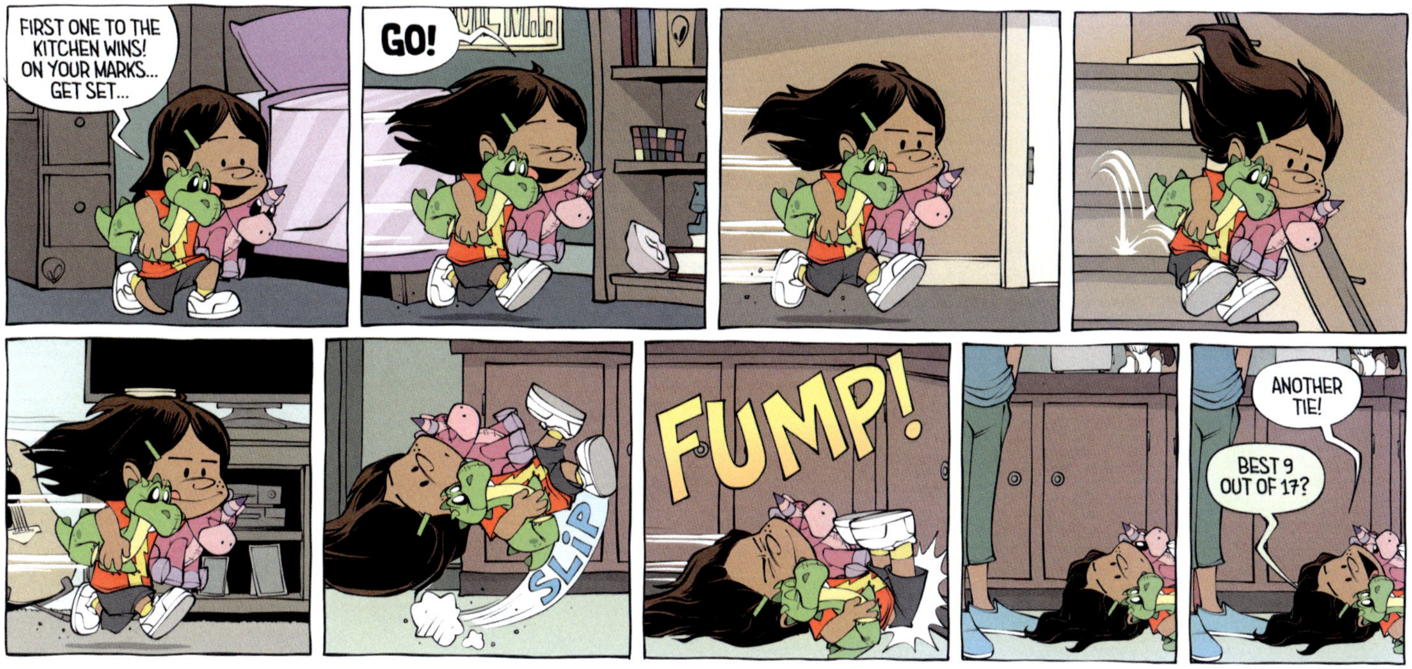
FIRST ONE TO THE KITCHEN WINS! ON YOUR MARKS... GET SET...
GO!
SLIP
FUMP!
ANOTHER TIE!
BEST 9 OUT OF 17?

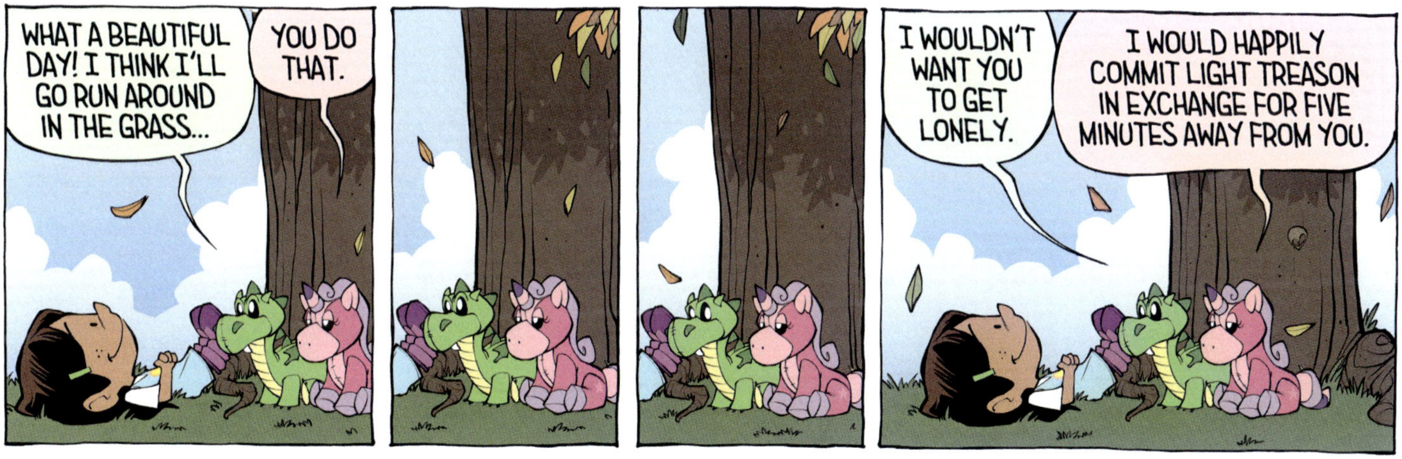
WHAT A BEAUTIFUL DAY! I THINK I'LL GO RUN AROUND IN THE GRASS...
YOU DO THAT.
I WOULDN'T WANT YOU TO GET LONELY.
I WOULD HAPPILY COMMIT LIGHT TREASON IN EXCHANGE FOR FIVE MINUTES AWAY FROM YOU.

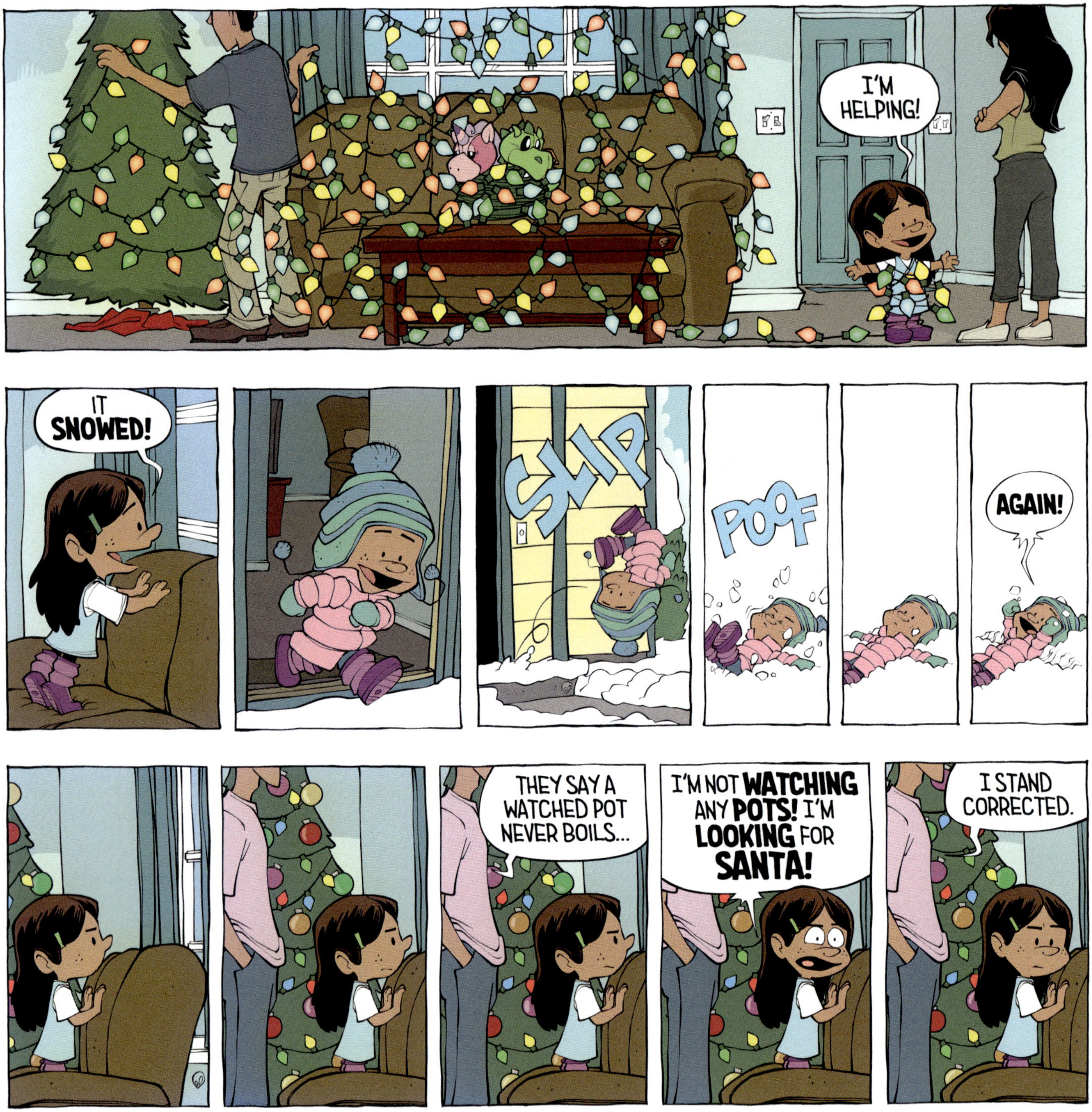
I'M HELPING!
IT SNOWED!
SLIP
POOF
AGAIN!
THEY SAY A WATCHED POT NEVER BOILS...
I'M NOT WATCHING ANY POTS! I'M LOOKING FOR SANTA!
I STAND CORRECTED.

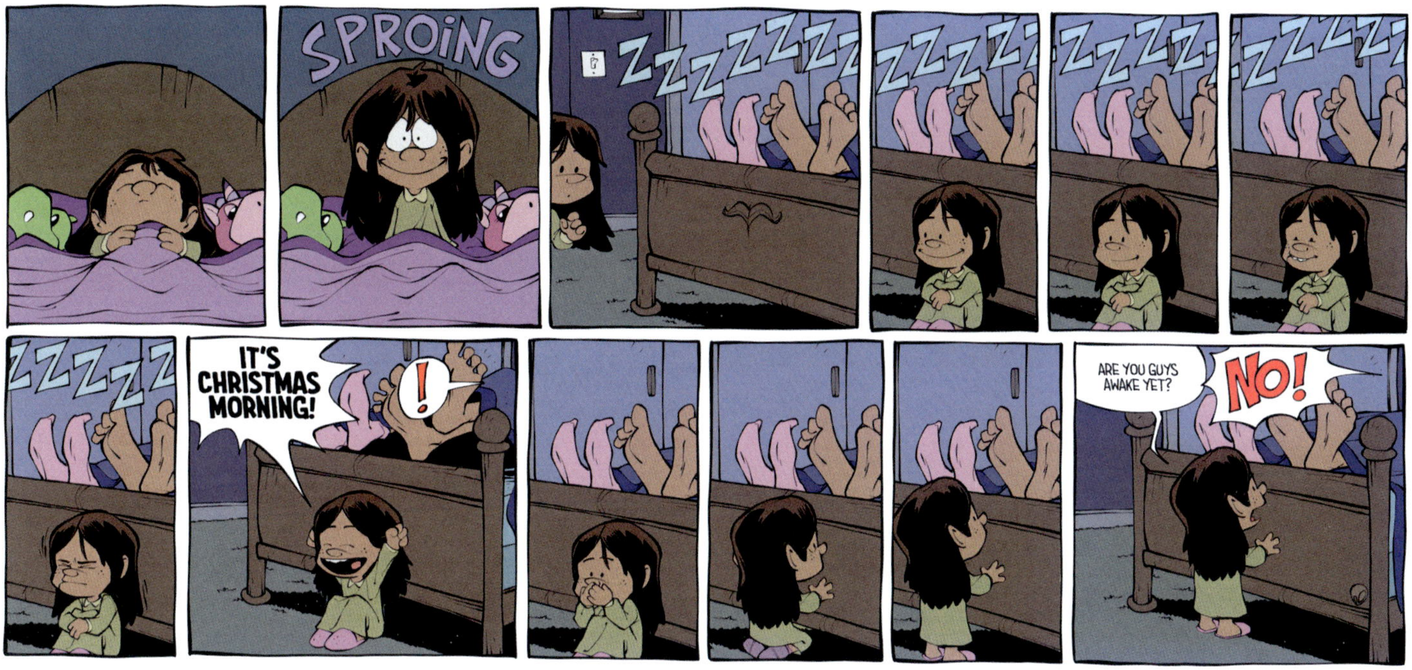
SPROING
IT'S CHRISTMAS MORNING!
!
ARE YOU GUYS AWAKE YET?
NO!

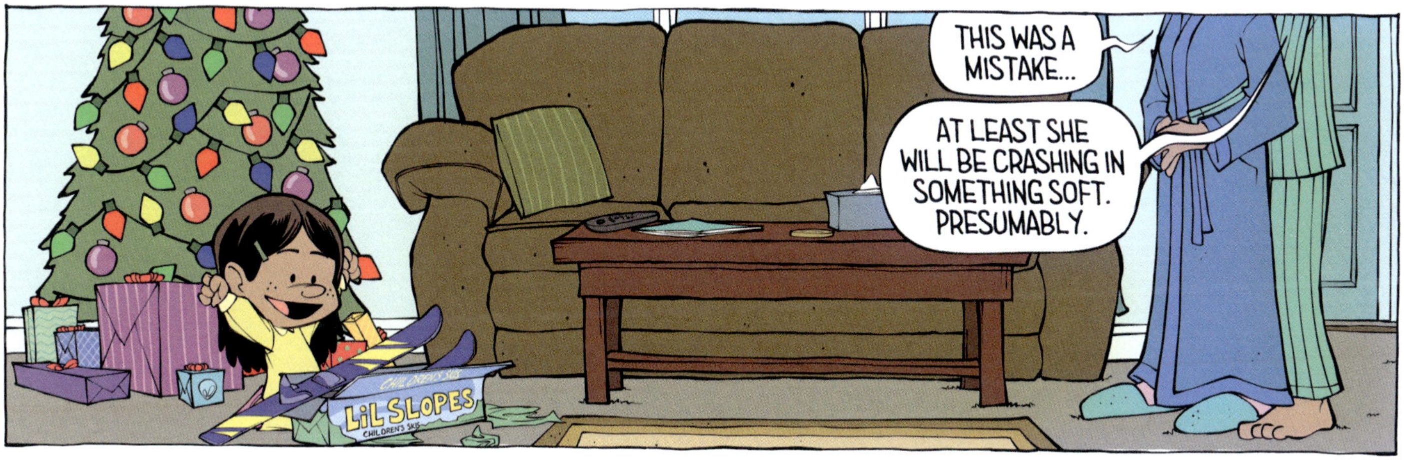
THIS WAS A MISTAKE...
AT LEAST SHE WILL BE CRASHING IN SOMETHING SOFT. PRESUMABLY.
LiL SLOPES
CHILDREN'S SKIS

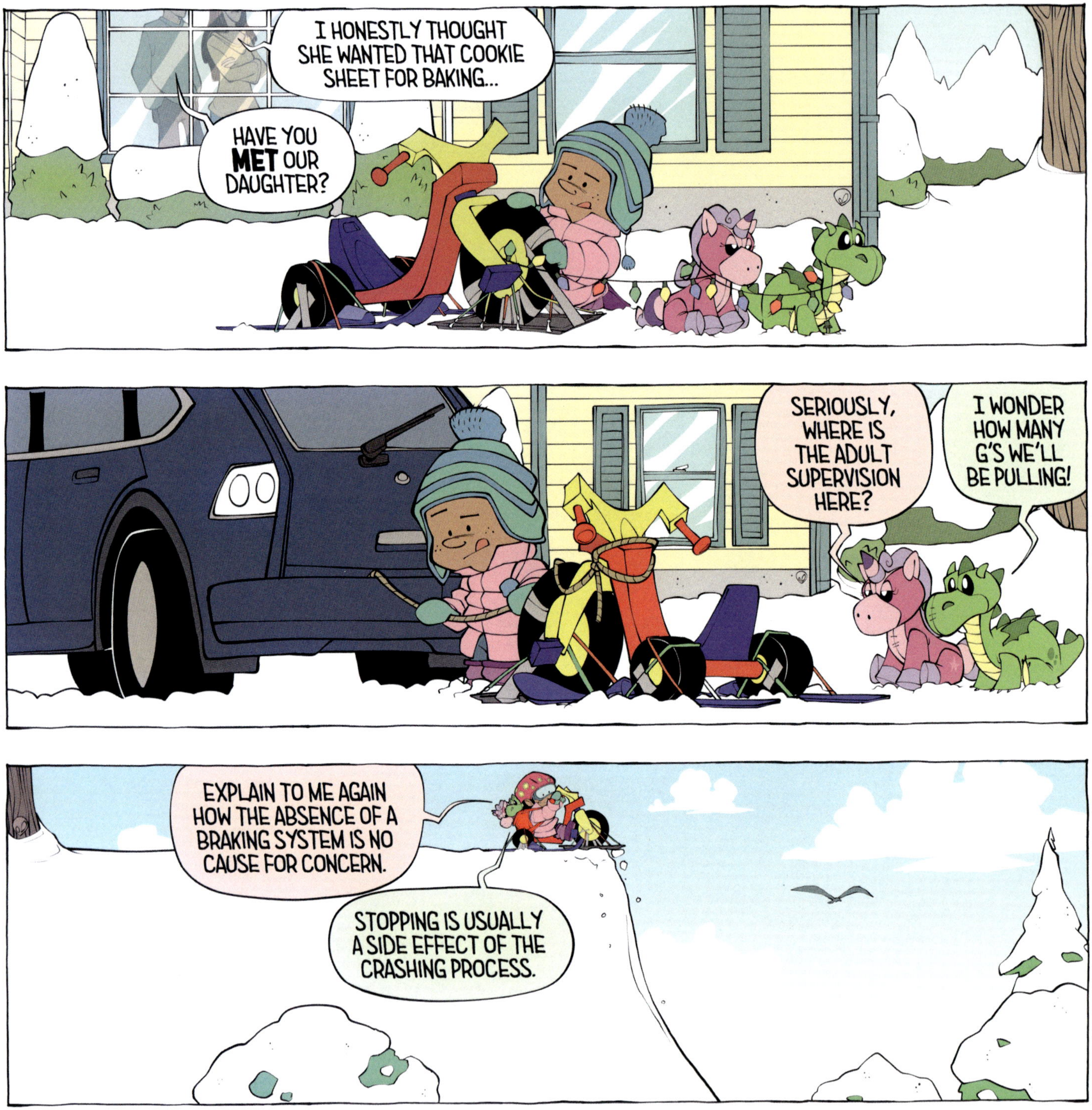
I HONESTLY THOUGHT SHE WANTED THAT COOKIE SHEET FOR BAKING...
HAVE YOU **MET** OUR DAUGHTER?
SERIOUSLY, WHERE IS THE ADULT SUPERVISION HERE?
I WONDER HOW MANY G'S WE'LL BE PULLING!
EXPLAIN TO ME AGAIN HOW THE ABSENCE OF A BRAKING SYSTEM IS NO CAUSE FOR CONCERN.
STOPPING IS USUALLY A SIDE EFFECT OF THE CRASHING PROCESS.

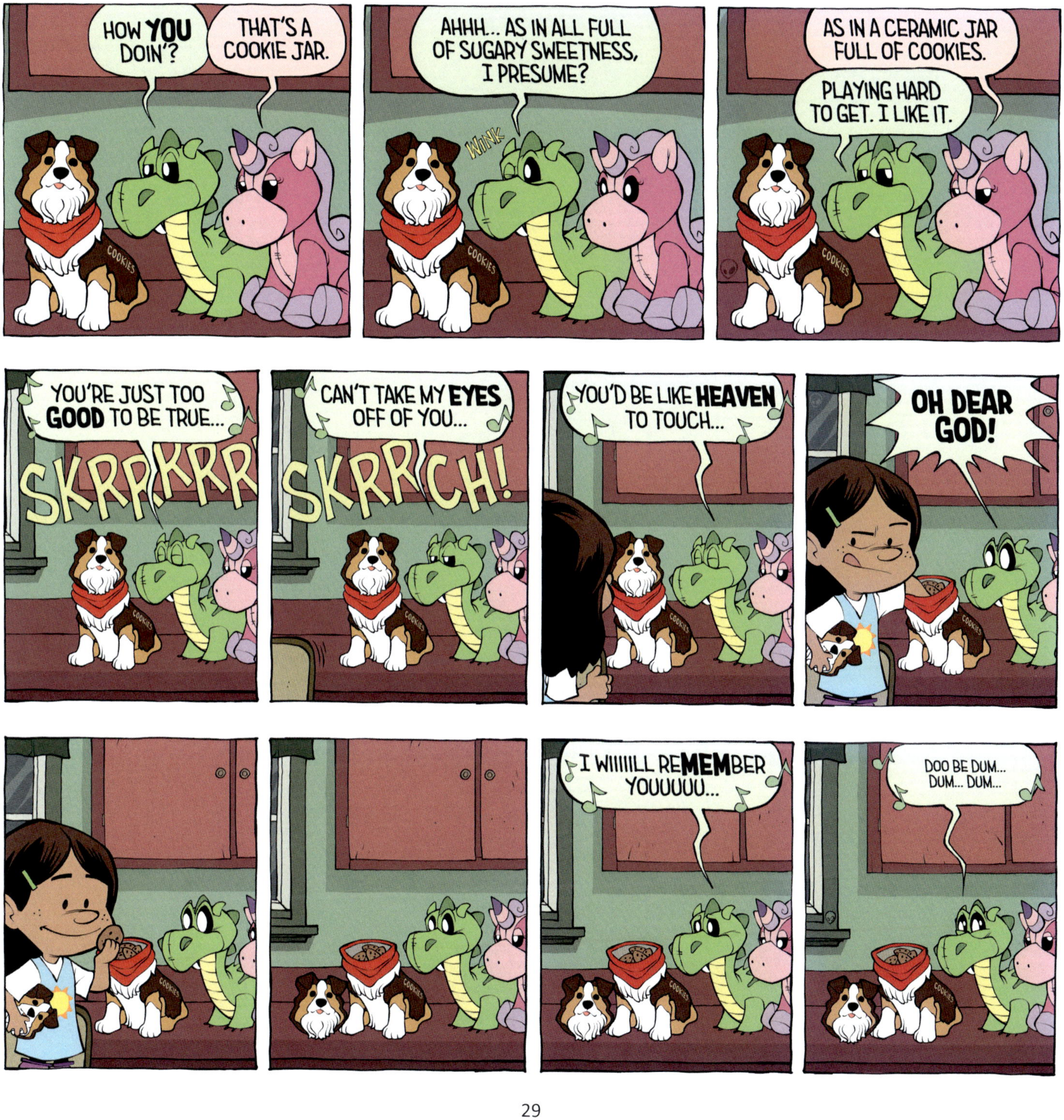
HOW YOU DOIN'?
THAT'S A COOKIE JAR.
AHHH... AS IN ALL FULL OF SUGARY SWEETNESS, I PRESUME?
WINK
AS IN A CERAMIC JAR FULL OF COOKIES.
PLAYING HARD TO GET. I LIKE IT.
YOU'RE JUST TOO GOOD TO BE TRUE...
SKRRKRR
CAN'T TAKE MY EYES OFF OF YOU...
SKRRCH!
YOU'D BE LIKE HEAVEN TO TOUCH...
OH DEAR GOD!
I WIIIIILL REMEMBER YOUUUUU...
DOO BE DUM... DUM... DUM...

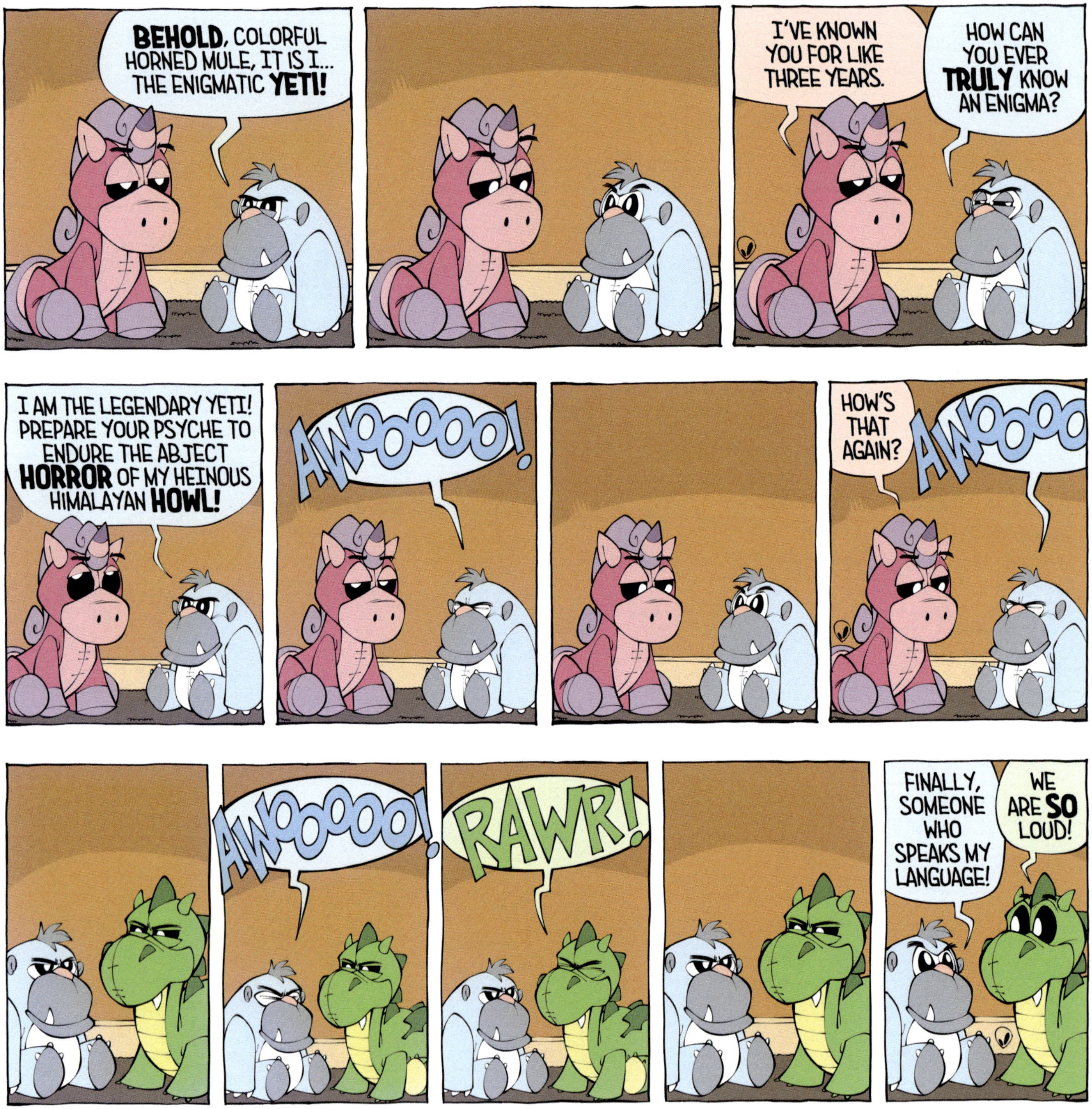
BEHOLD, COLORFUL HORNED MULE, IT IS I... THE ENIGMATIC YETI!
I'VE KNOWN YOU FOR LIKE THREE YEARS.
HOW CAN YOU EVER TRULY KNOW AN ENIGMA?
I AM THE LEGENDARY YETI! PREPARE YOUR PSYCHE TO ENDURE THE ABJECT HORROR OF MY HEINOUS HIMALAYAN HOWL!
AWOOOOO!
HOW'S THAT AGAIN?
AWOOOO
AWOOOOO!
RAWR!
FINALLY, SOMEONE WHO SPEAKS MY LANGUAGE!
WE ARE SO LOUD!

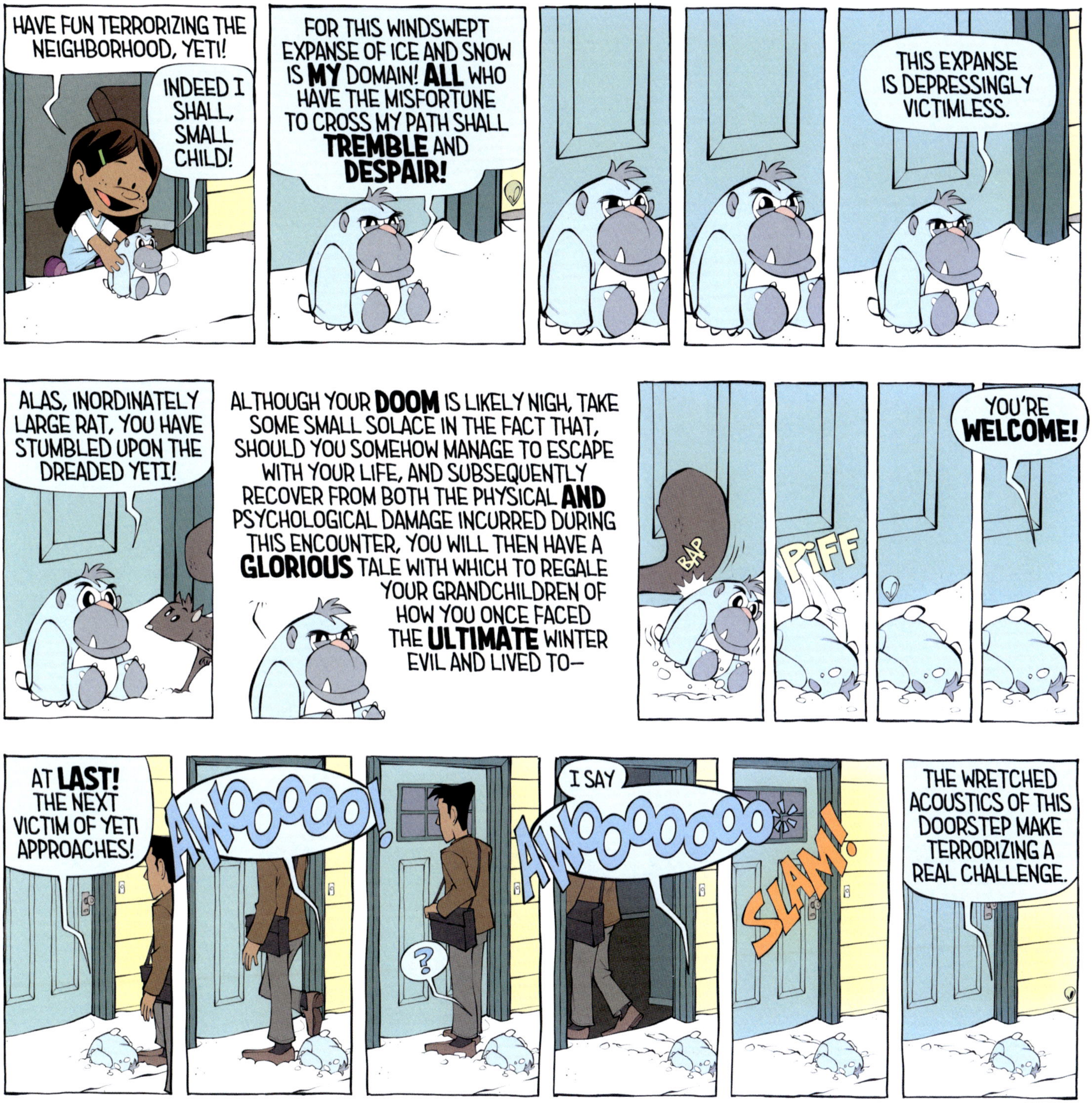
HAVE FUN TERRORIZING THE NEIGHBORHOOD, YETI!
INDEED I SHALL, SMALL CHILD!
FOR THIS WINDSWEPT EXPANSE OF ICE AND SNOW IS **MY** DOMAIN! **ALL** WHO HAVE THE MISFORTUNE TO CROSS MY PATH SHALL **TREMBLE** AND **DESPAIR!**
THIS EXPANSE IS DEPRESSINGLY VICTIMLESS.
ALAS, INORDINATELY LARGE RAT, YOU HAVE STUMBLED UPON THE DREADED YETI!
ALTHOUGH YOUR **DOOM** IS LIKELY NIGH, TAKE SOME SMALL SOLACE IN THE FACT THAT, SHOULD YOU SOMEHOW MANAGE TO ESCAPE WITH YOUR LIFE, AND SUBSEQUENTLY RECOVER FROM BOTH THE PHYSICAL **AND** PSYCHOLOGICAL DAMAGE INCURRED DURING THIS ENCOUNTER, YOU WILL THEN HAVE A **GLORIOUS** TALE WITH WHICH TO REGALE YOUR GRANDCHILDREN OF HOW YOU ONCE FACED THE **ULTIMATE** WINTER EVIL AND LIVED TO—
BAP
PIFF
YOU'RE **WELCOME!**
AT **LAST!** THE NEXT VICTIM OF YETI APPROACHES!
AWOOOOO!
?
I SAY
AWOOOOOOOO
SLAM!
THE WRETCHED ACOUSTICS OF THIS DOORSTEP MAKE TERRORIZING A REAL CHALLENGE.

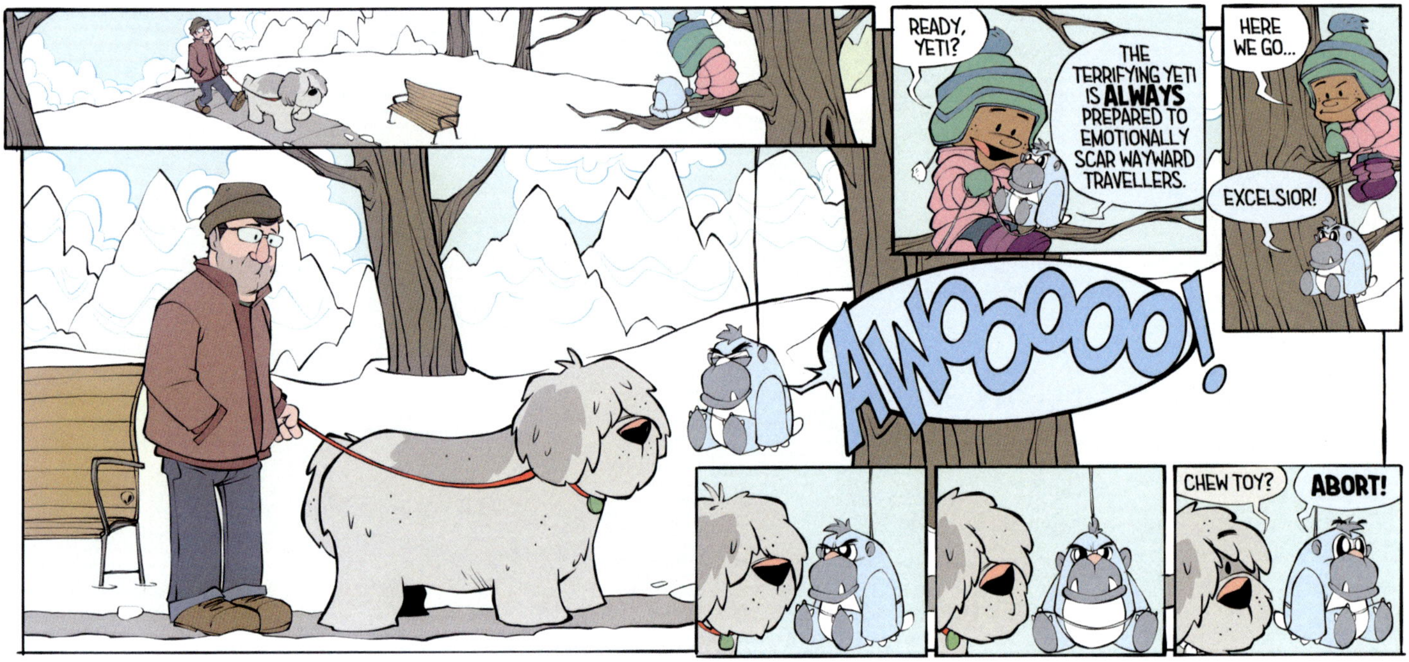
READY, YETI?
THE TERRIFYING YETI IS **ALWAYS** PREPARED TO EMOTIONALLY SCAR WAYWARD TRAVELLERS.
HERE WE GO...
EXCELSIOR!
AWOOOOO!
CHEW TOY?
ABORT!

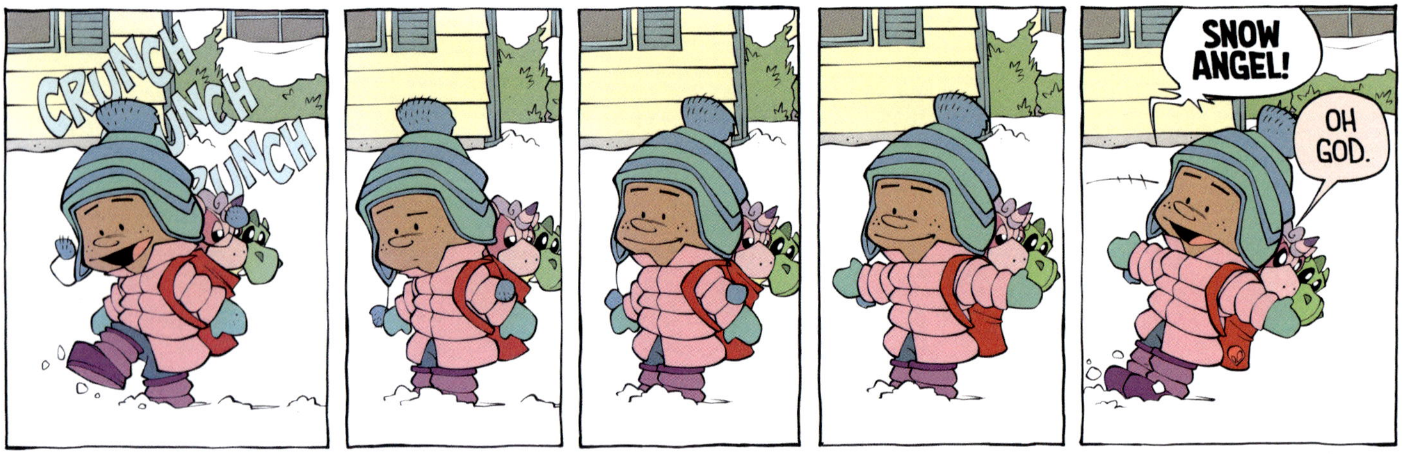
CRUNCH
UNCH
UNCH
SNOW ANGEL!
OH GOD.

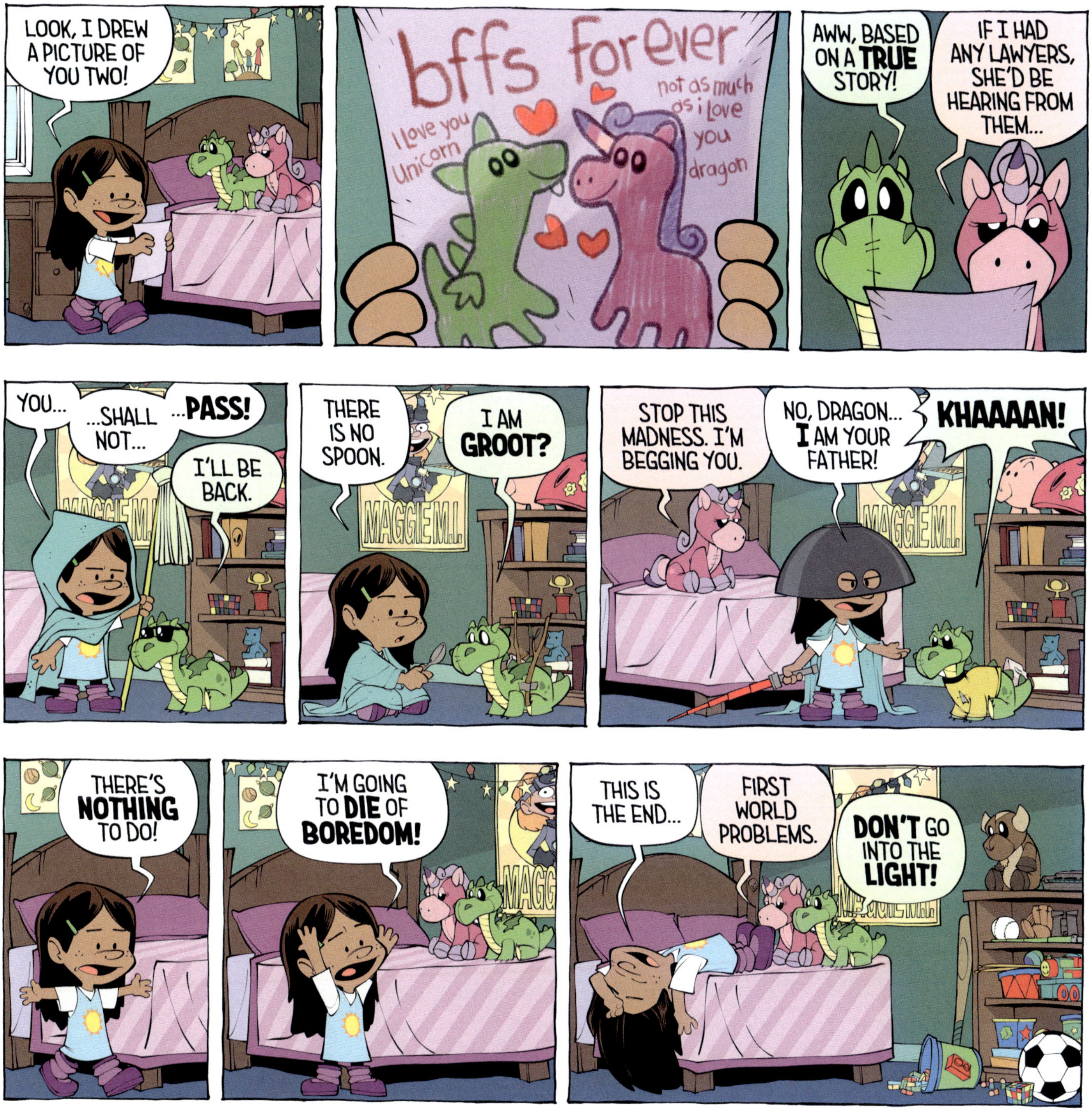
LOOK, I DREW A PICTURE OF YOU TWO!
bffs forever
I Love you Unicorn
not as much as i Love you dragon
AWW, BASED ON A **TRUE** STORY!
IF I HAD ANY LAWYERS, SHE'D BE HEARING FROM THEM...
YOU...
...SHALL NOT...
...**PASS!**
I'LL BE BACK.
MAGGIE M.I.
THERE IS NO SPOON.
I AM **GROOT?**
STOP THIS MADNESS. I'M BEGGING YOU.
NO, DRAGON... **I** AM YOUR FATHER!
KHAAAAN!
THERE'S **NOTHING** TO DO!
I'M GOING TO **DIE** OF **BOREDOM!**
THIS IS THE END...
FIRST WORLD PROBLEMS.
DON'T GO INTO THE **LIGHT!**

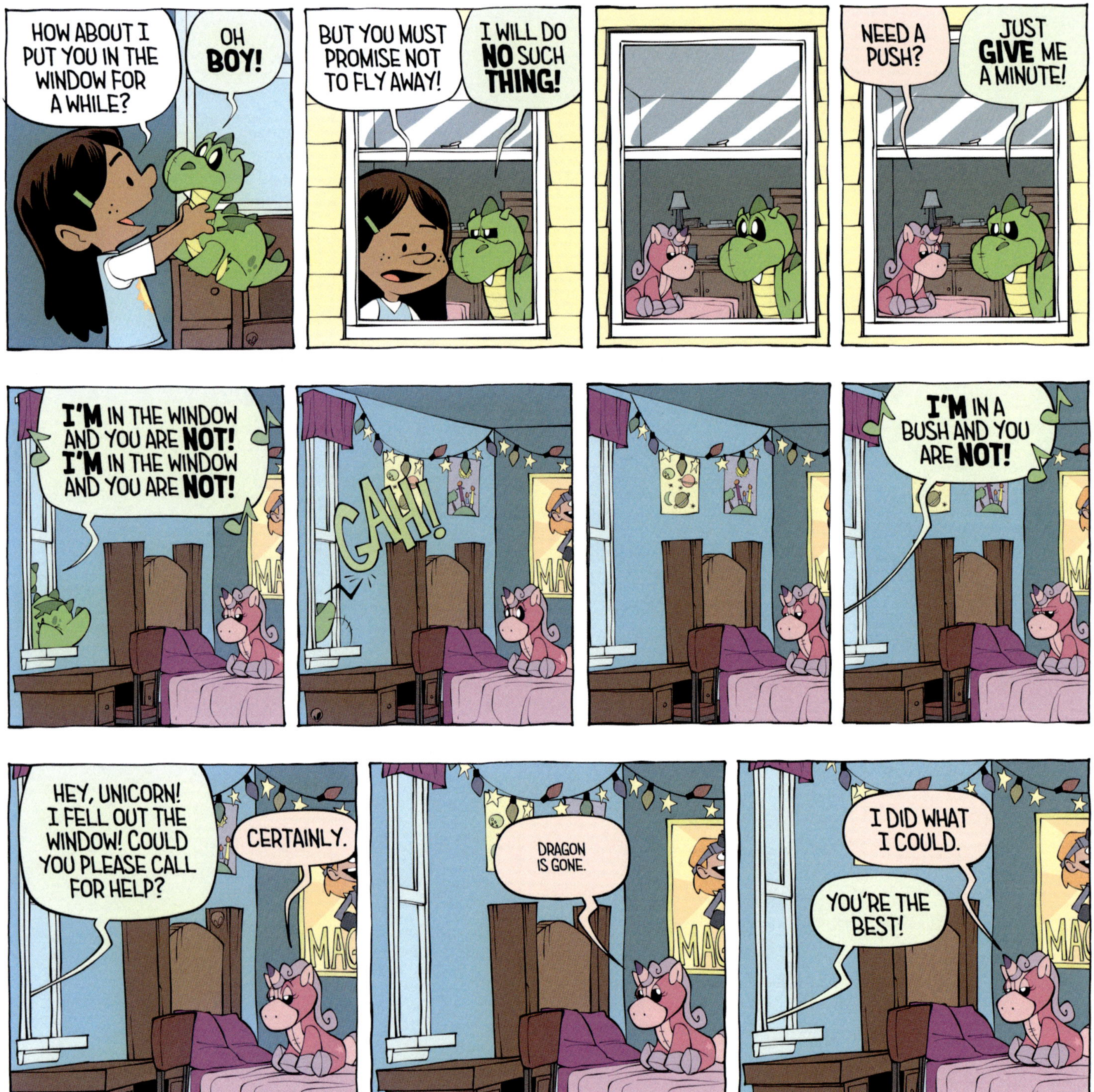
HOW ABOUT I PUT YOU IN THE WINDOW FOR A WHILE?
OH **BOY!**
BUT YOU MUST PROMISE NOT TO FLY AWAY!
I WILL DO **NO** SUCH **THING!**
NEED A PUSH?
JUST **GIVE** ME A MINUTE!
I'M IN THE WINDOW AND YOU ARE **NOT! I'M** IN THE WINDOW AND YOU ARE **NOT!**
GAH!
I'M IN A BUSH AND YOU ARE **NOT!**
HEY, UNICORN! I FELL OUT THE WINDOW! COULD YOU PLEASE CALL FOR HELP?
CERTAINLY.
DRAGON IS GONE.
I DID WHAT I COULD.
YOU'RE THE BEST!

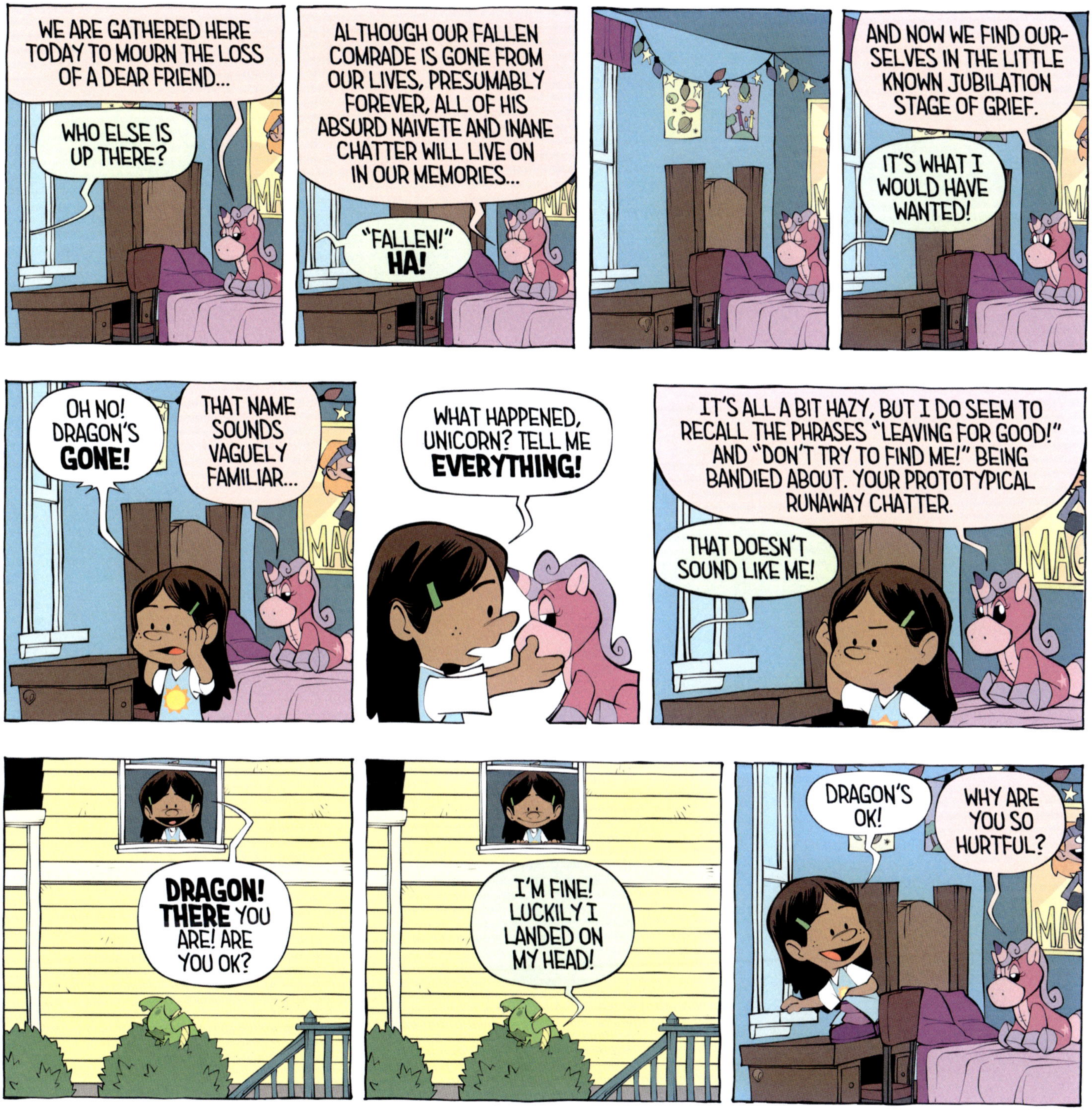
WE ARE GATHERED HERE TODAY TO MOURN THE LOSS OF A DEAR FRIEND...
WHO ELSE IS UP THERE?
ALTHOUGH OUR FALLEN COMRADE IS GONE FROM OUR LIVES, PRESUMABLY FOREVER, ALL OF HIS ABSURD NAIVETE AND INANE CHATTER WILL LIVE ON IN OUR MEMORIES...
"FALLEN!" HA!
AND NOW WE FIND OURSELVES IN THE LITTLE KNOWN JUBILATION STAGE OF GRIEF.
IT'S WHAT I WOULD HAVE WANTED!
OH NO! DRAGON'S GONE!
THAT NAME SOUNDS VAGUELY FAMILIAR...
WHAT HAPPENED, UNICORN? TELL ME EVERYTHING!
IT'S ALL A BIT HAZY, BUT I DO SEEM TO RECALL THE PHRASES "LEAVING FOR GOOD!" AND "DON'T TRY TO FIND ME!" BEING BANDIED ABOUT. YOUR PROTOTYPICAL RUNAWAY CHATTER.
THAT DOESN'T SOUND LIKE ME!
DRAGON! THERE YOU ARE! ARE YOU OK?
I'M FINE! LUCKILY I LANDED ON MY HEAD!
DRAGON'S OK!
WHY ARE YOU SO HURTFUL?

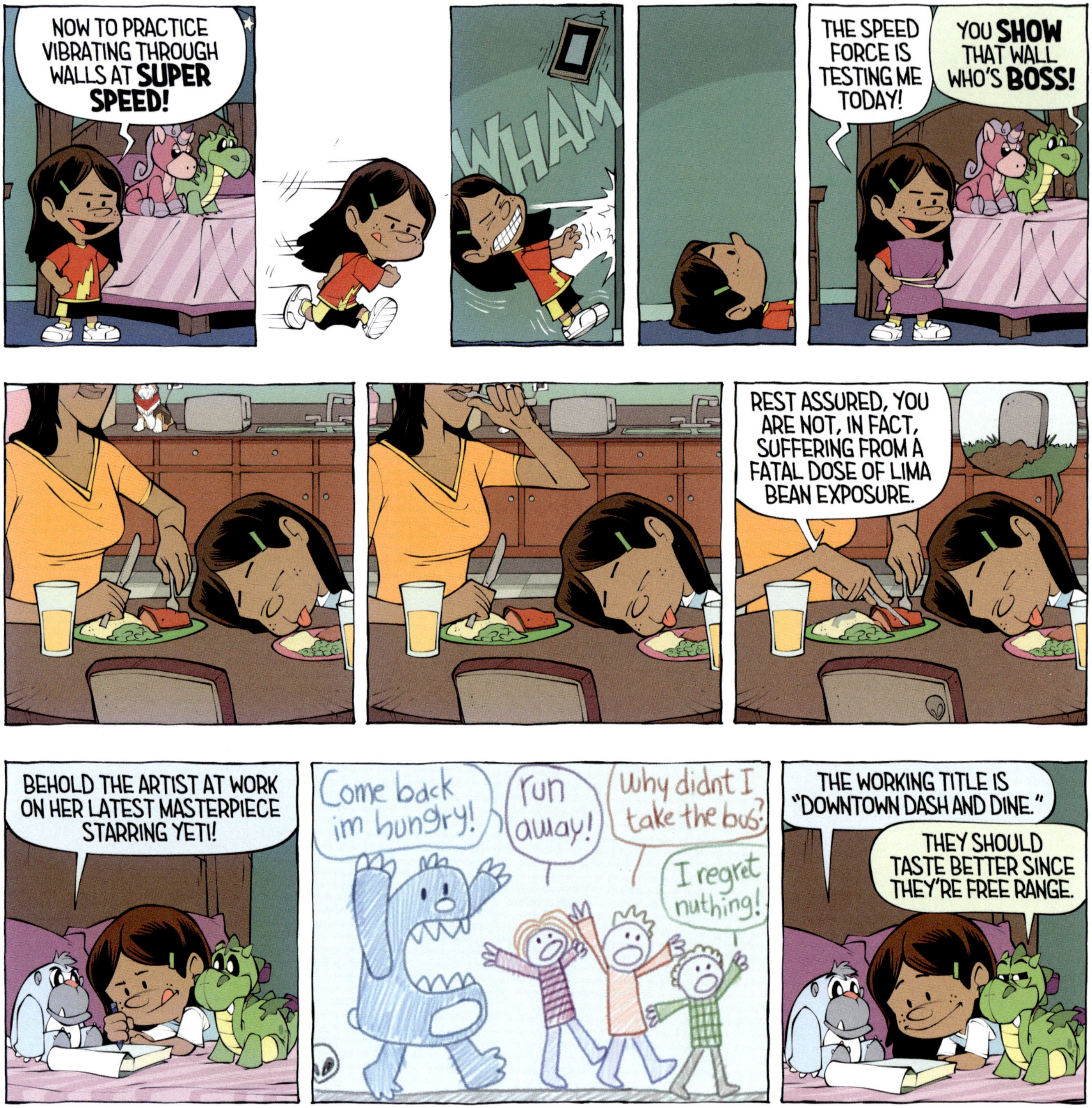
NOW TO PRACTICE VIBRATING THROUGH WALLS AT SUPER SPEED!
WHAM
THE SPEED FORCE IS TESTING ME TODAY!
YOU SHOW THAT WALL WHO'S BOSS!
REST ASSURED, YOU ARE NOT, IN FACT, SUFFERING FROM A FATAL DOSE OF LIMA BEAN EXPOSURE.
BEHOLD THE ARTIST AT WORK ON HER LATEST MASTERPIECE STARRING YETI!
Come back im hungry!
run away!
Why didnt I take the bus?
I regret nuthing!
THE WORKING TITLE IS "DOWNTOWN DASH AND DINE."
THEY SHOULD TASTE BETTER SINCE THEY'RE FREE RANGE.

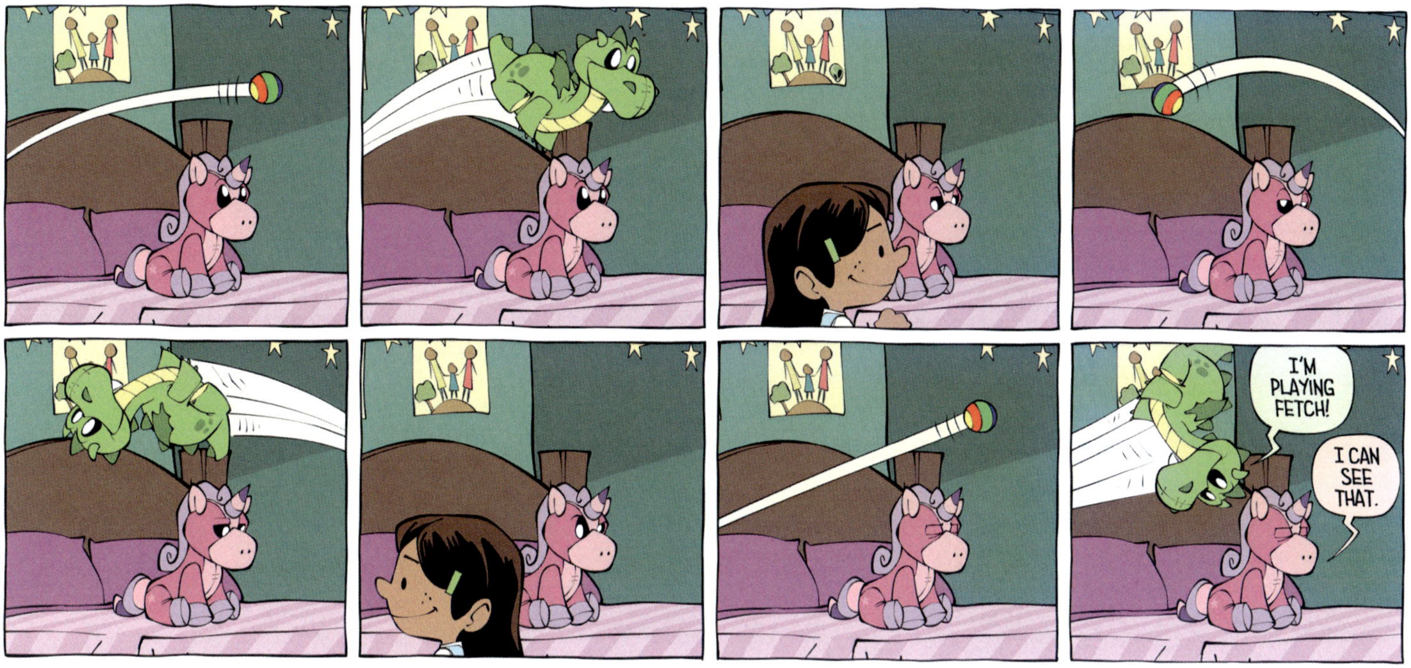
I'M PLAYING FETCH!
I CAN SEE THAT.

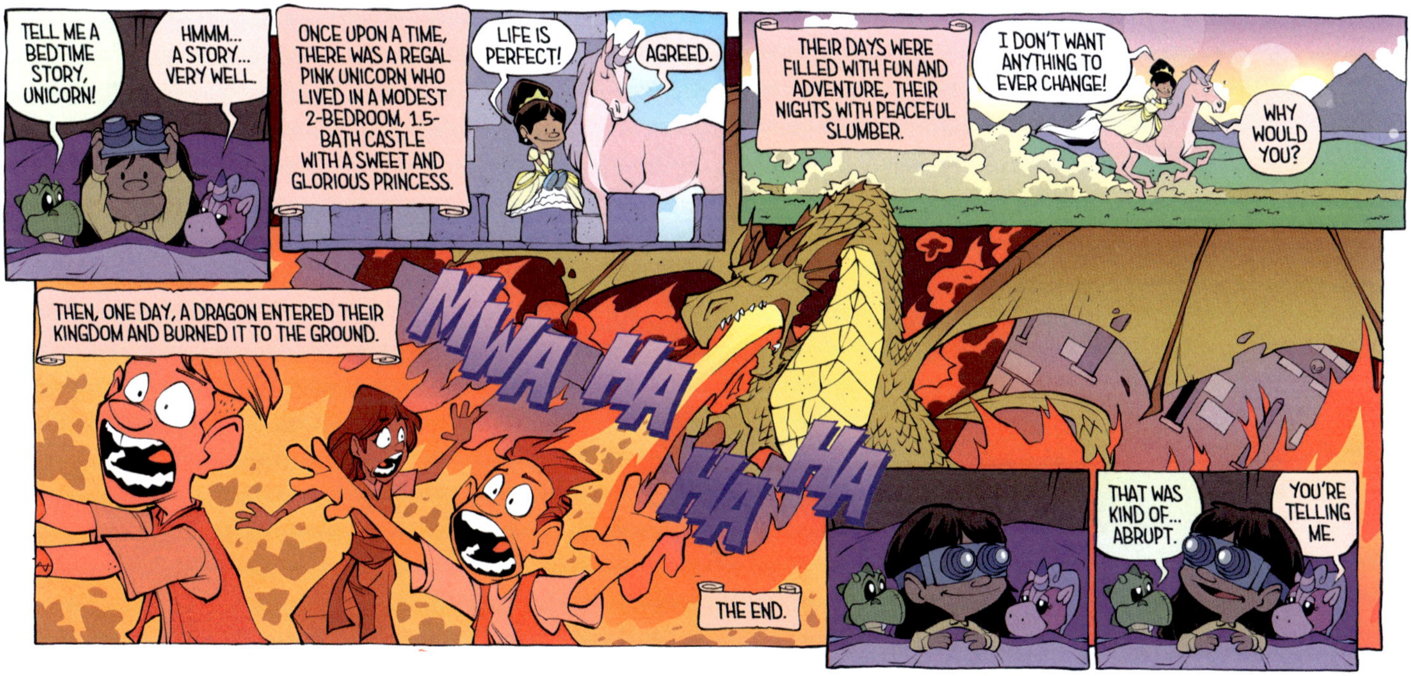
TELL ME A BEDTIME STORY, UNICORN!
HMMM... A STORY... VERY WELL.
ONCE UPON A TIME, THERE WAS A REGAL PINK UNICORN WHO LIVED IN A MODEST 2-BEDROOM, 1.5-BATH CASTLE WITH A SWEET AND GLORIOUS PRINCESS.
LIFE IS PERFECT!
AGREED.
THEIR DAYS WERE FILLED WITH FUN AND ADVENTURE, THEIR NIGHTS WITH PEACEFUL SLUMBER.
I DON'T WANT ANYTHING TO EVER CHANGE!
WHY WOULD YOU?
THEN, ONE DAY, A DRAGON ENTERED THEIR KINGDOM AND BURNED IT TO THE GROUND.
MWA HA HA HA HA
THE END.
THAT WAS KIND OF... ABRUPT.
YOU'RE TELLING ME.

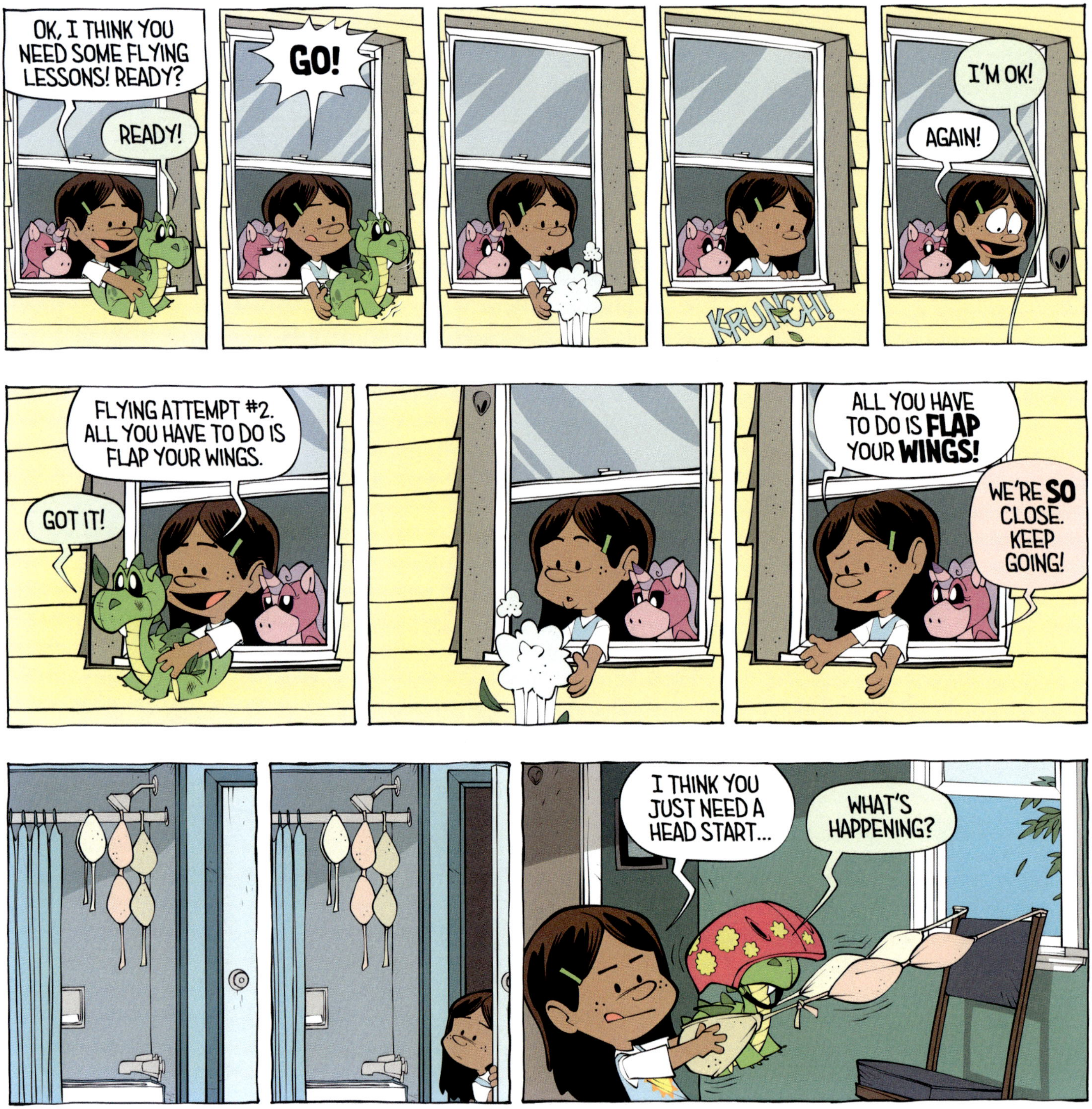
OK, I THINK YOU NEED SOME FLYING LESSONS! READY?
READY!
GO!
KRUNCH!
I'M OK!
AGAIN!
FLYING ATTEMPT #2. ALL YOU HAVE TO DO IS FLAP YOUR WINGS.
GOT IT!
ALL YOU HAVE TO DO IS FLAP YOUR WINGS!
WE'RE SO CLOSE. KEEP GOING!
I THINK YOU JUST NEED A HEAD START...
WHAT'S HAPPENING?

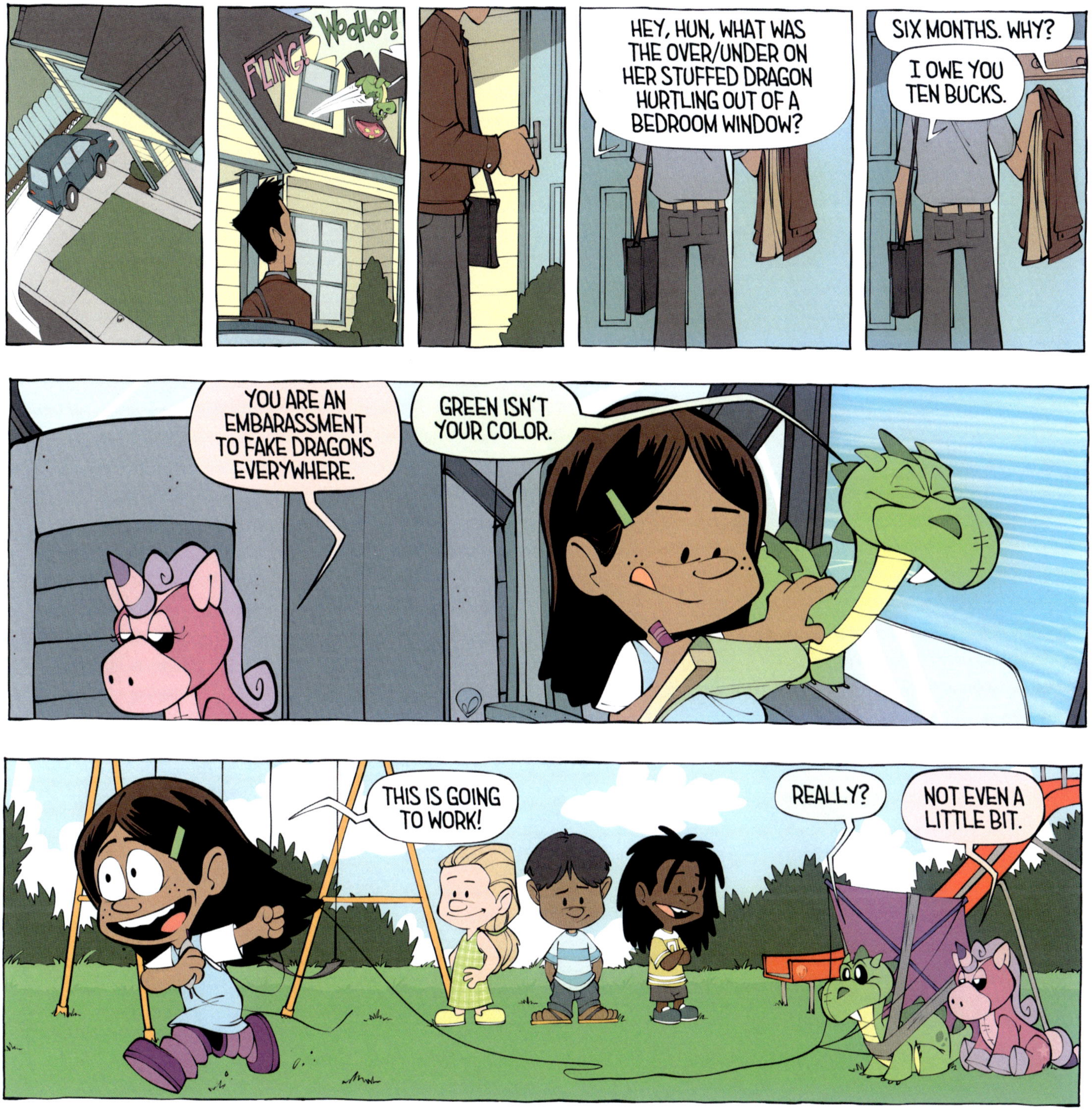
FLING!
WOOHOO!
HEY, HUN, WHAT WAS THE OVER/UNDER ON HER STUFFED DRAGON HURTLING OUT OF A BEDROOM WINDOW?
SIX MONTHS. WHY?
I OWE YOU TEN BUCKS.
YOU ARE AN EMBARASSMENT TO FAKE DRAGONS EVERYWHERE.
GREEN ISN'T YOUR COLOR.
THIS IS GOING TO WORK!
REALLY?
NOT EVEN A LITTLE BIT.

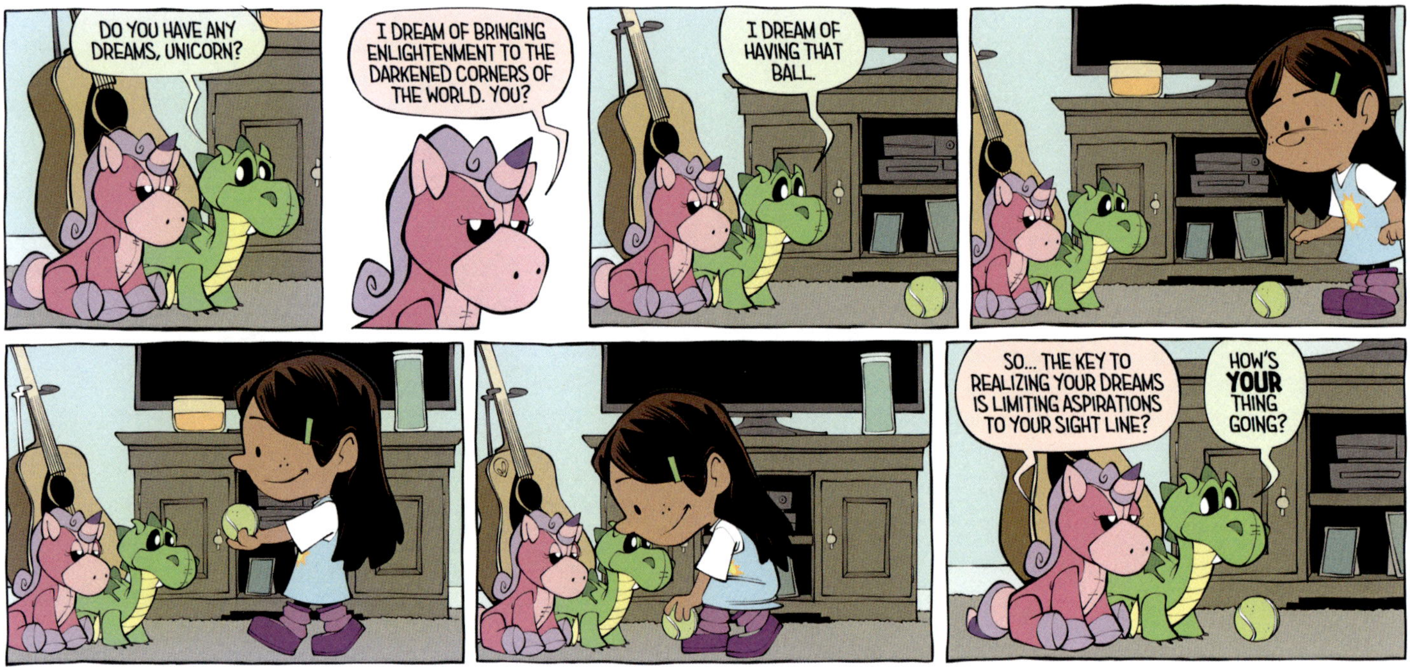
DO YOU HAVE ANY DREAMS, UNICORN?
I DREAM OF BRINGING ENLIGHTENMENT TO THE DARKENED CORNERS OF THE WORLD. YOU?
I DREAM OF HAVING THAT BALL.
SO... THE KEY TO REALIZING YOUR DREAMS IS LIMITING ASPIRATIONS TO YOUR SIGHT LINE?
HOW'S **YOUR** THING GOING?

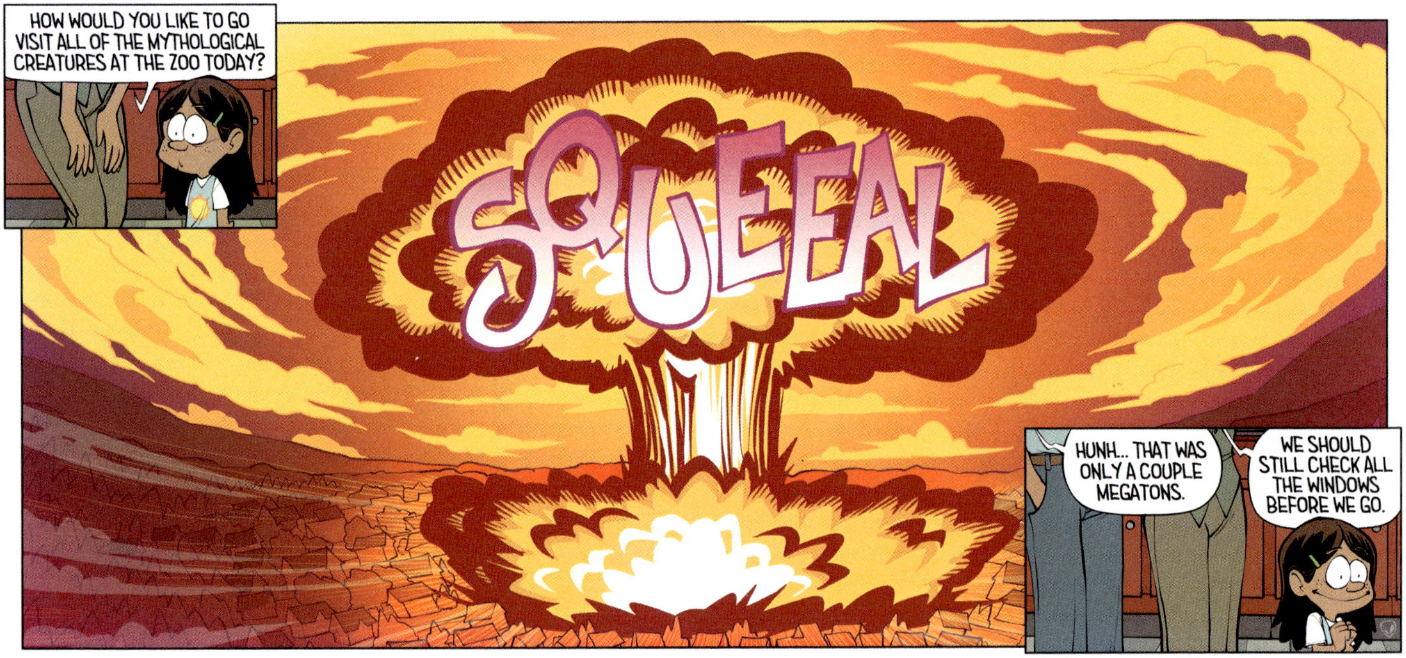
HOW WOULD YOU LIKE TO GO VISIT ALL OF THE MYTHOLOGICAL CREATURES AT THE ZOO TODAY?
SQUEEAL
HUNH... THAT WAS ONLY A COUPLE MEGATONS.
WE SHOULD STILL CHECK ALL THE WINDOWS BEFORE WE GO.

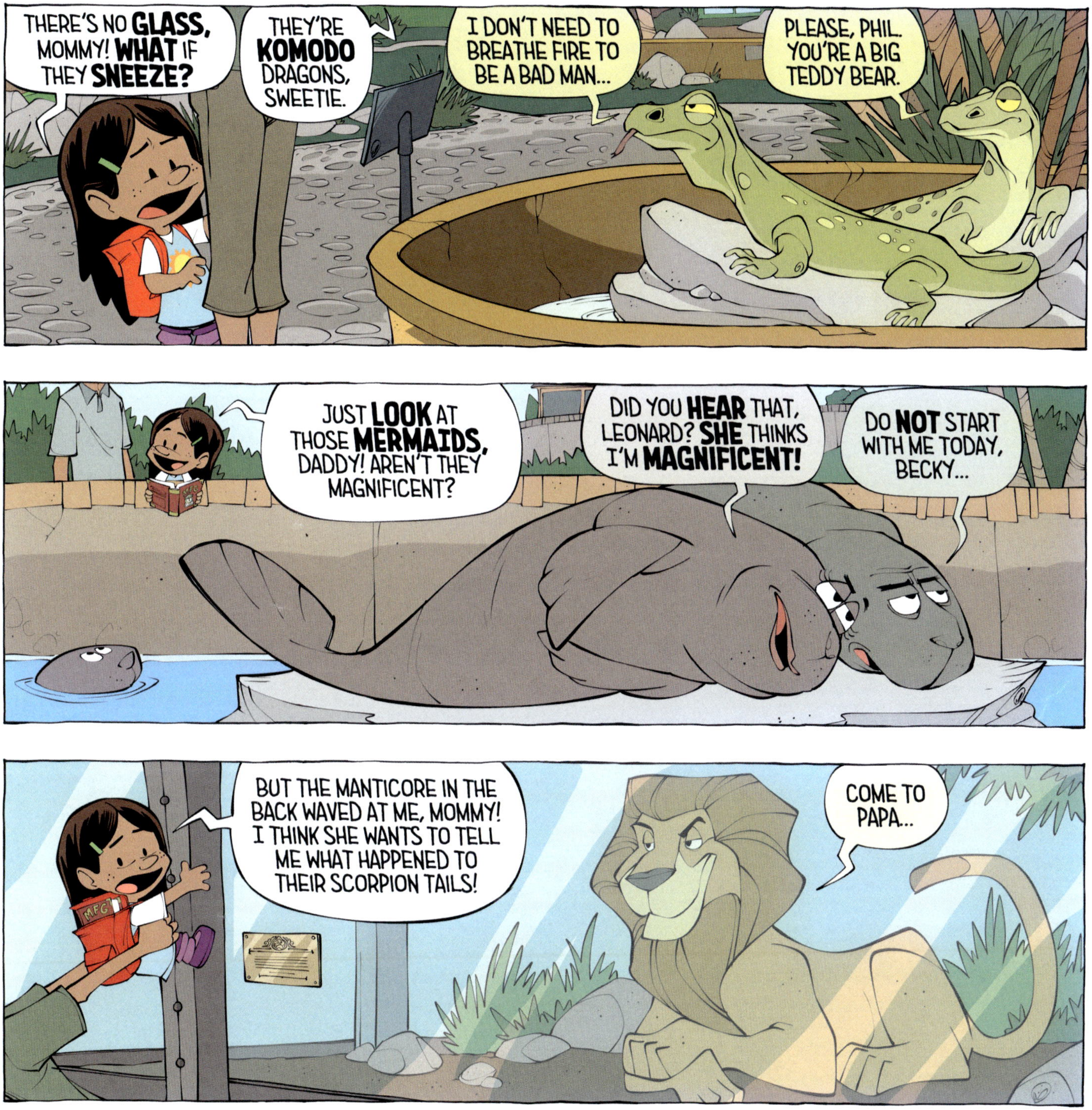
THERE'S NO GLASS, MOMMY! WHAT IF THEY SNEEZE?
THEY'RE KOMODO DRAGONS, SWEETIE.
I DON'T NEED TO BREATHE FIRE TO BE A BAD MAN...
PLEASE, PHIL. YOU'RE A BIG TEDDY BEAR.
JUST LOOK AT THOSE MERMAIDS, DADDY! AREN'T THEY MAGNIFICENT?
DID YOU HEAR THAT, LEONARD? SHE THINKS I'M MAGNIFICENT!
DO NOT START WITH ME TODAY, BECKY...
BUT THE MANTICORE IN THE BACK WAVED AT ME, MOMMY! I THINK SHE WANTS TO TELL ME WHAT HAPPENED TO THEIR SCORPION TAILS!
COME TO PAPA...

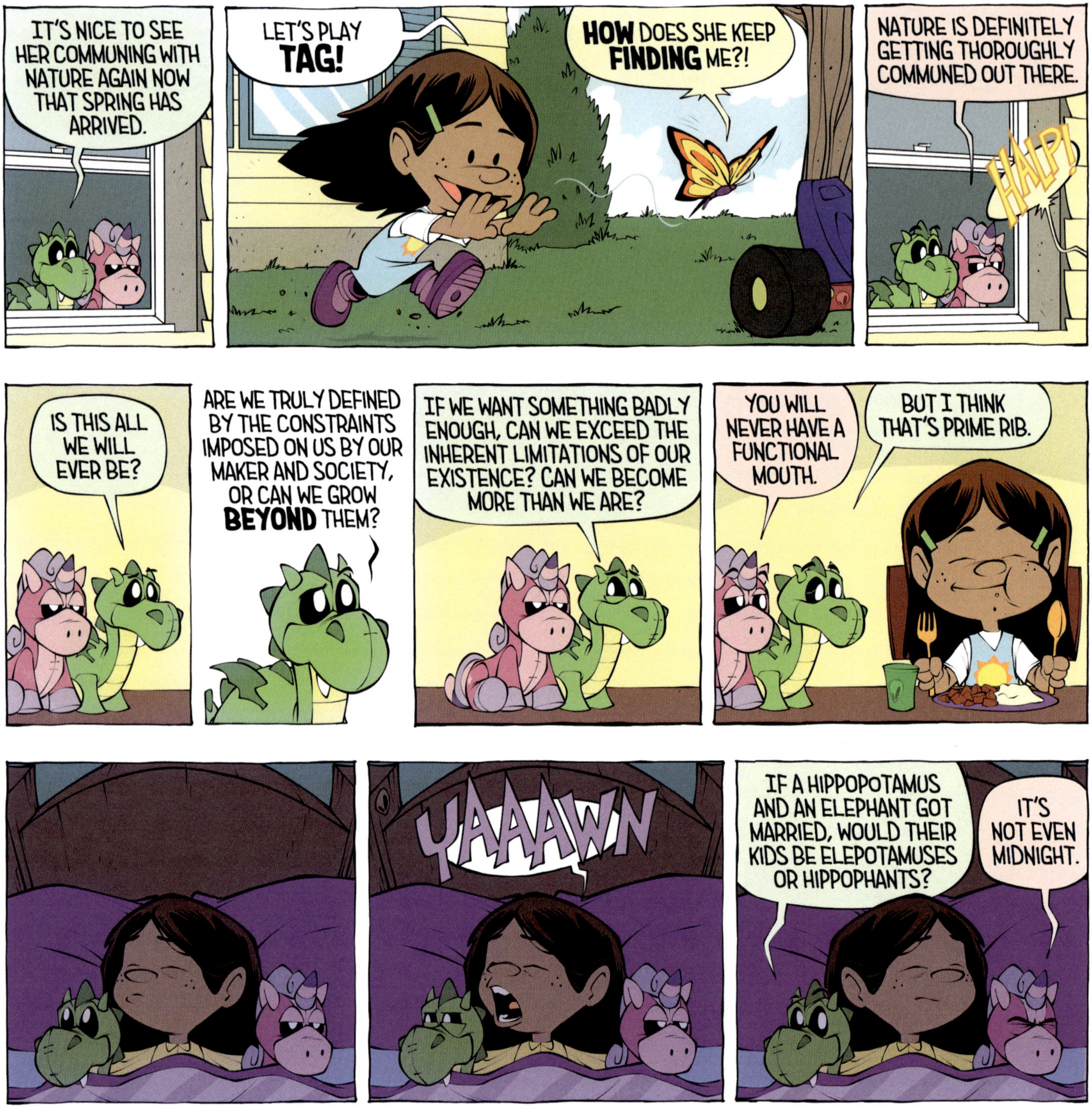
IT'S NICE TO SEE HER COMMUNING WITH NATURE AGAIN NOW THAT SPRING HAS ARRIVED.
LET'S PLAY **TAG!**
HOW DOES SHE KEEP **FINDING** ME?!
NATURE IS DEFINITELY GETTING THOROUGHLY COMMUNED OUT THERE.
HALP!
IS THIS ALL WE WILL EVER BE?
ARE WE TRULY DEFINED BY THE CONSTRAINTS IMPOSED ON US BY OUR MAKER AND SOCIETY, OR CAN WE GROW **BEYOND** THEM?
IF WE WANT SOMETHING BADLY ENOUGH, CAN WE EXCEED THE INHERENT LIMITATIONS OF OUR EXISTENCE? CAN WE BECOME MORE THAN WE ARE?
YOU WILL NEVER HAVE A FUNCTIONAL MOUTH.
BUT I THINK THAT'S PRIME RIB.
YAAAWN
IF A HIPPOPOTAMUS AND AN ELEPHANT GOT MARRIED, WOULD THEIR KIDS BE ELEPOTAMUSES OR HIPPOPHANTS?
IT'S NOT EVEN MIDNIGHT.

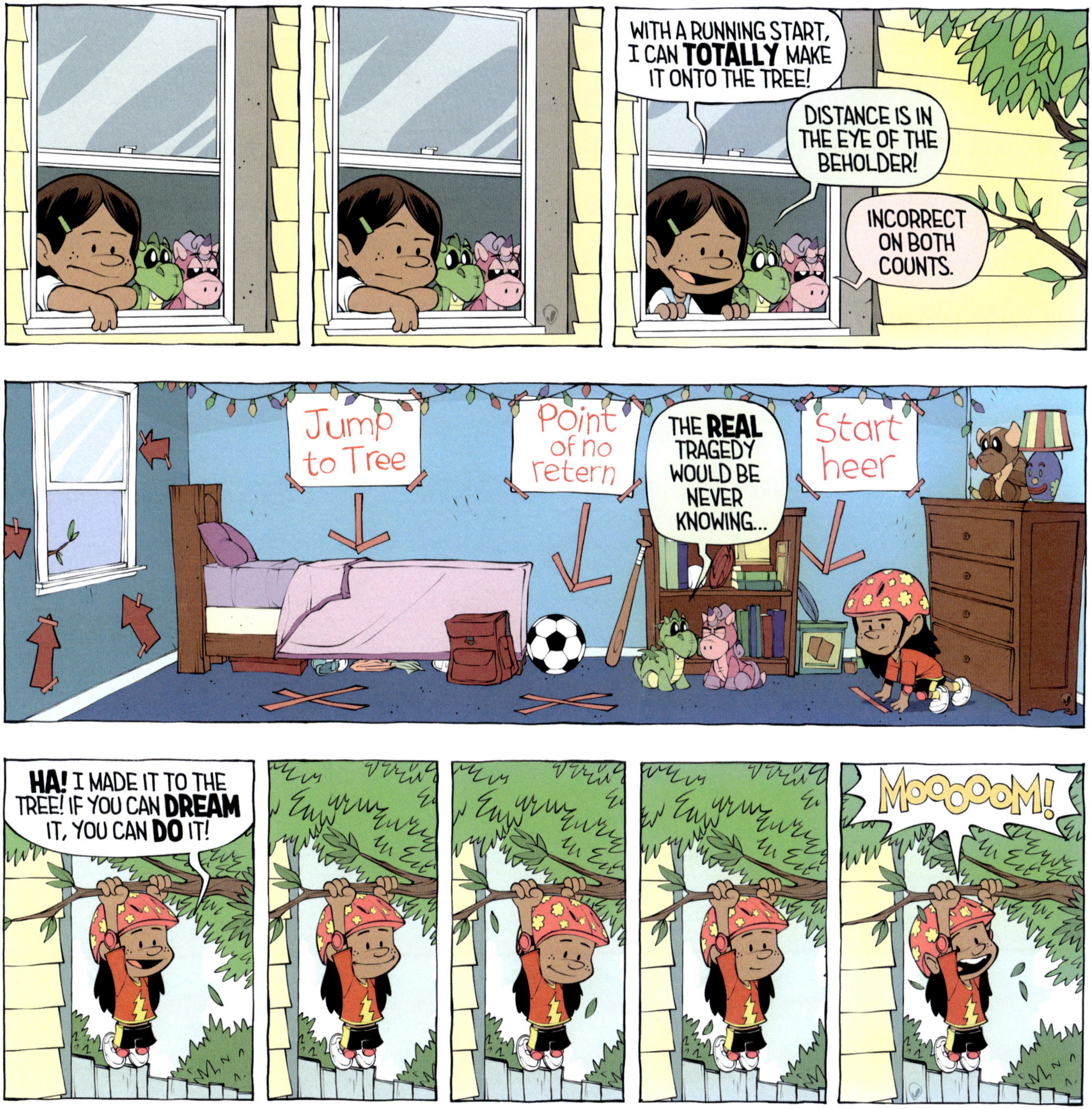
WITH A RUNNING START, I CAN TOTALLY MAKE IT ONTO THE TREE!
DISTANCE IS IN THE EYE OF THE BEHOLDER!
INCORRECT ON BOTH COUNTS.
Jump to Tree
Point of no retern
THE REAL TRAGEDY WOULD BE NEVER KNOWING...
Start heer
HA! I MADE IT TO THE TREE! IF YOU CAN DREAM IT, YOU CAN DO IT!
MOOOOOM!

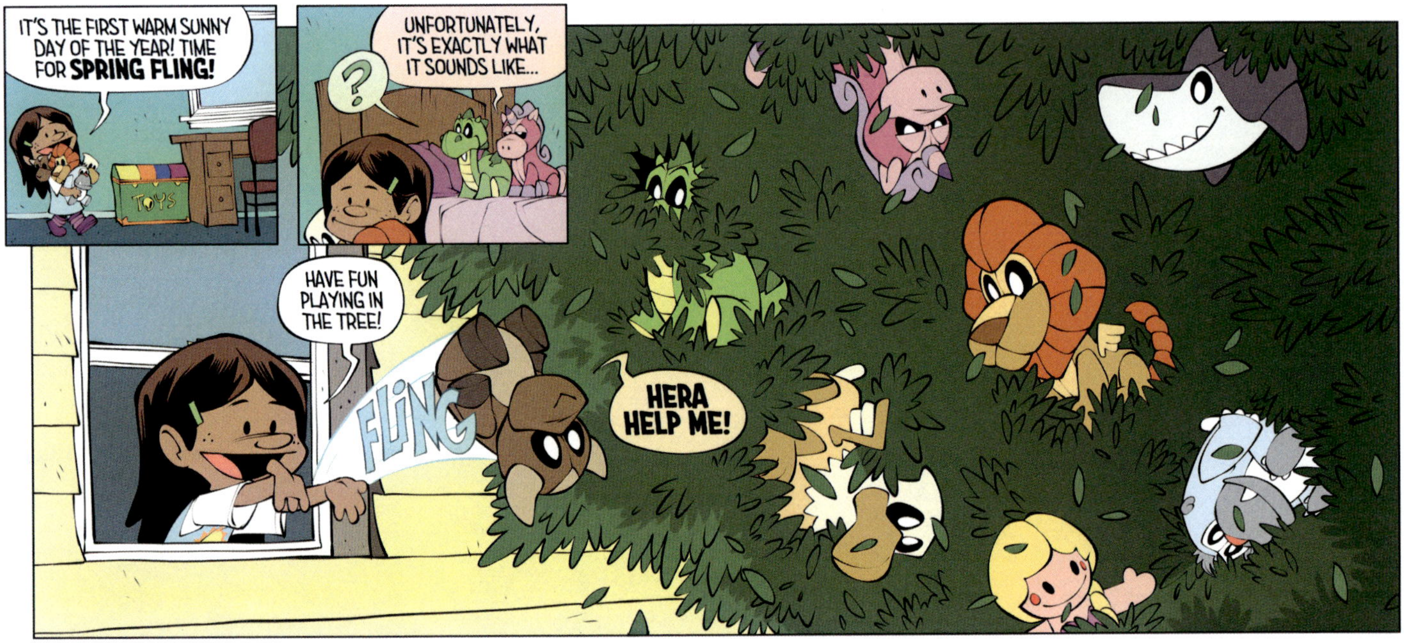
IT'S THE FIRST WARM SUNNY DAY OF THE YEAR! TIME FOR **SPRING FLING!**
TOYS
?
UNFORTUNATELY, IT'S EXACTLY WHAT IT SOUNDS LIKE...
HAVE FUN PLAYING IN THE TREE!
FLING
HERA HELP ME!

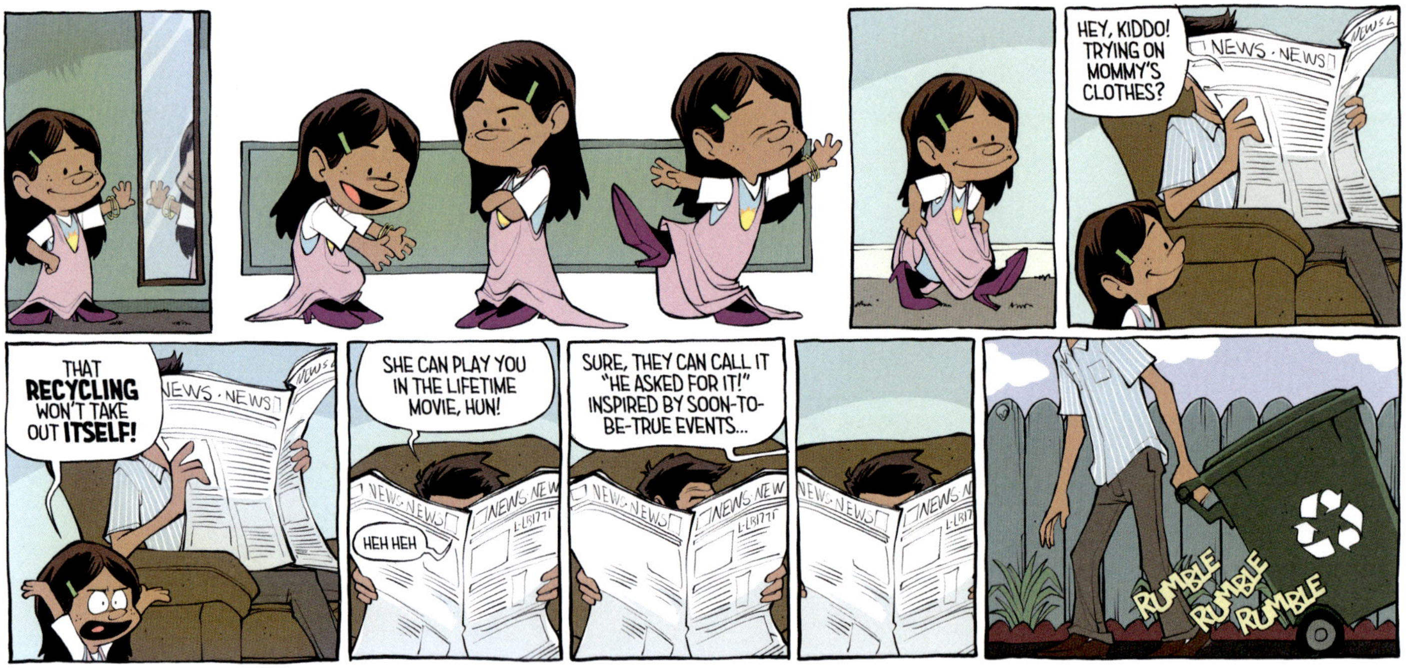
HEY, KIDDO! TRYING ON MOMMY'S CLOTHES?
NEWS · NEWS
THAT **RECYCLING** WON'T TAKE OUT **ITSELF!**
SHE CAN PLAY YOU IN THE LIFETIME MOVIE, HUN!
HEH HEH
SURE, THEY CAN CALL IT "HE ASKED FOR IT!" INSPIRED BY SOON-TO-BE-TRUE EVENTS...
RUMBLE RUMBLE RUMBLE

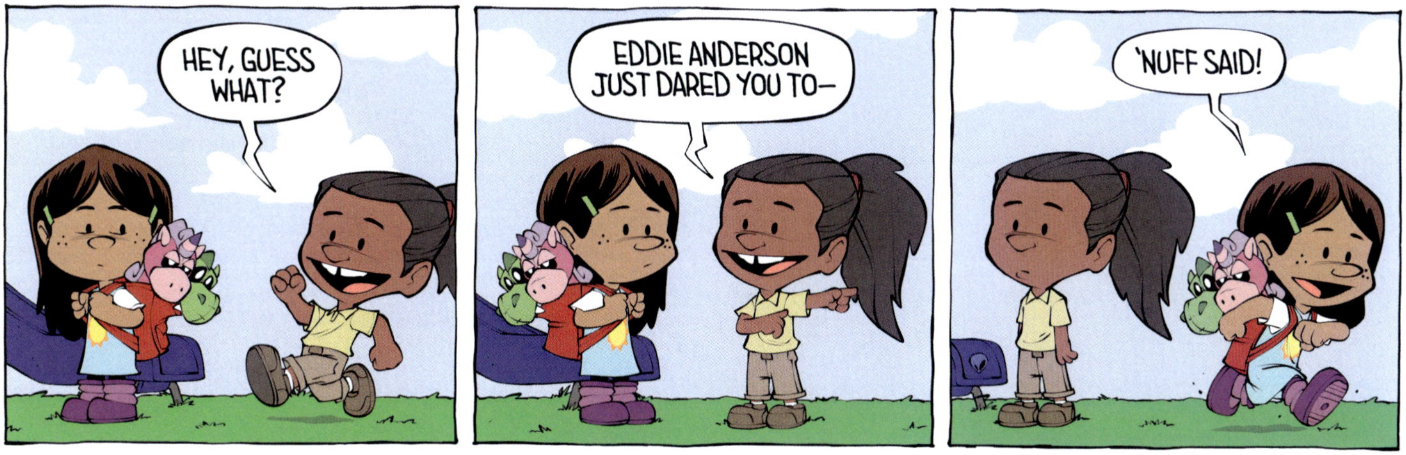
HEY, GUESS WHAT?
EDDIE ANDERSON JUST DARED YOU TO—
'NUFF SAID!

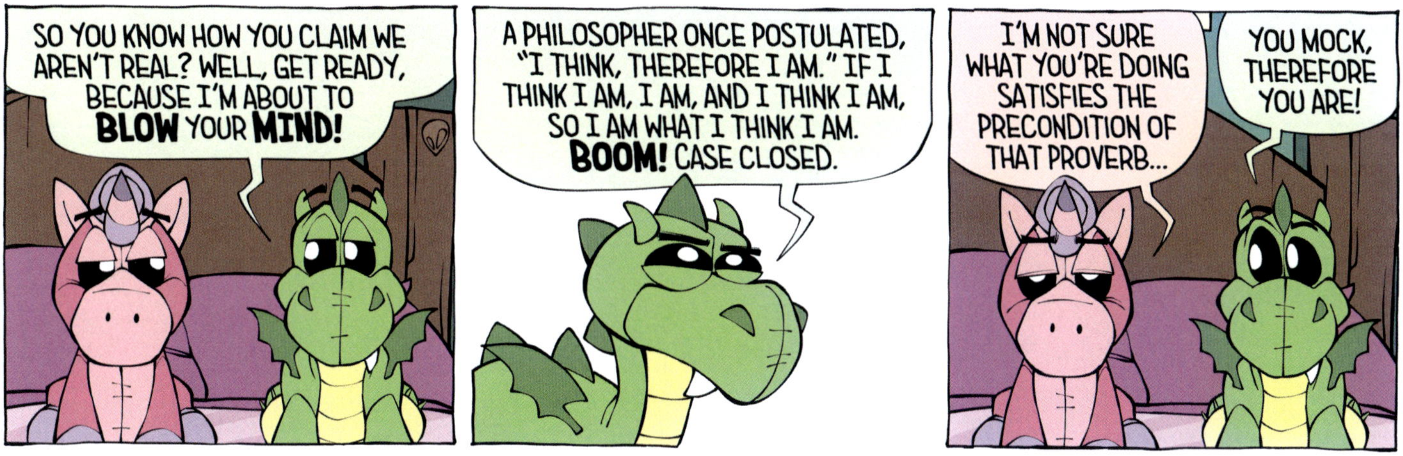
SO YOU KNOW HOW YOU CLAIM WE AREN'T REAL? WELL, GET READY, BECAUSE I'M ABOUT TO **BLOW** YOUR **MIND!**
A PHILOSOPHER ONCE POSTULATED, "I THINK, THEREFORE I AM." IF I THINK I AM, I AM, AND I THINK I AM, SO I AM WHAT I THINK I AM. **BOOM!** CASE CLOSED.
I'M NOT SURE WHAT YOU'RE DOING SATISFIES THE PRECONDITION OF THAT PROVERB...
YOU MOCK, THEREFORE YOU ARE!

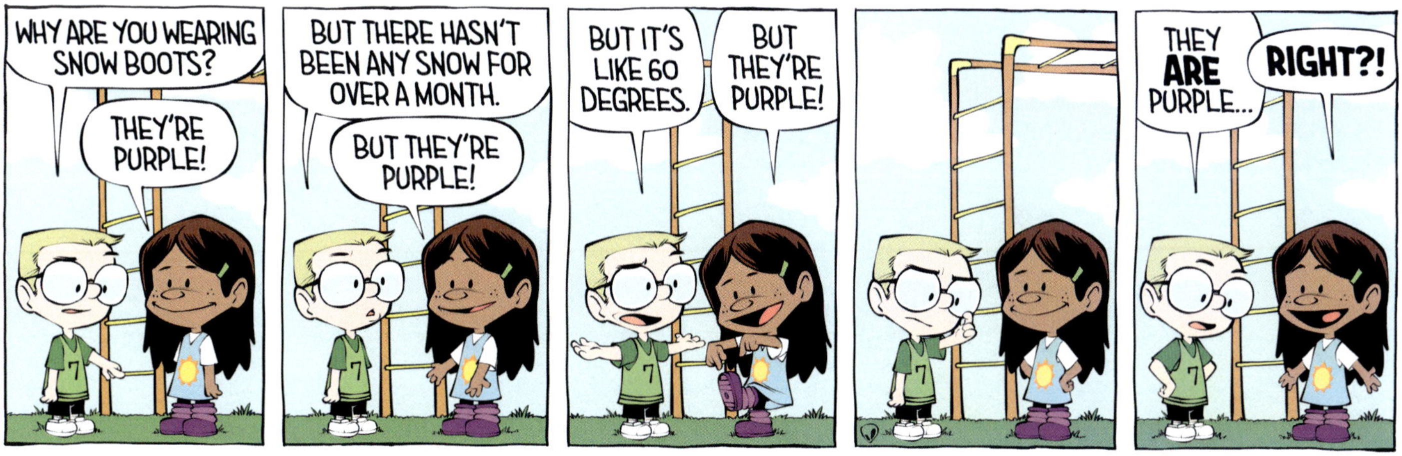
WHY ARE YOU WEARING SNOW BOOTS?
THEY'RE PURPLE!
BUT THERE HASN'T BEEN ANY SNOW FOR OVER A MONTH.
BUT THEY'RE PURPLE!
BUT IT'S LIKE 60 DEGREES.
BUT THEY'RE PURPLE!
THEY **ARE** PURPLE...
RIGHT?!

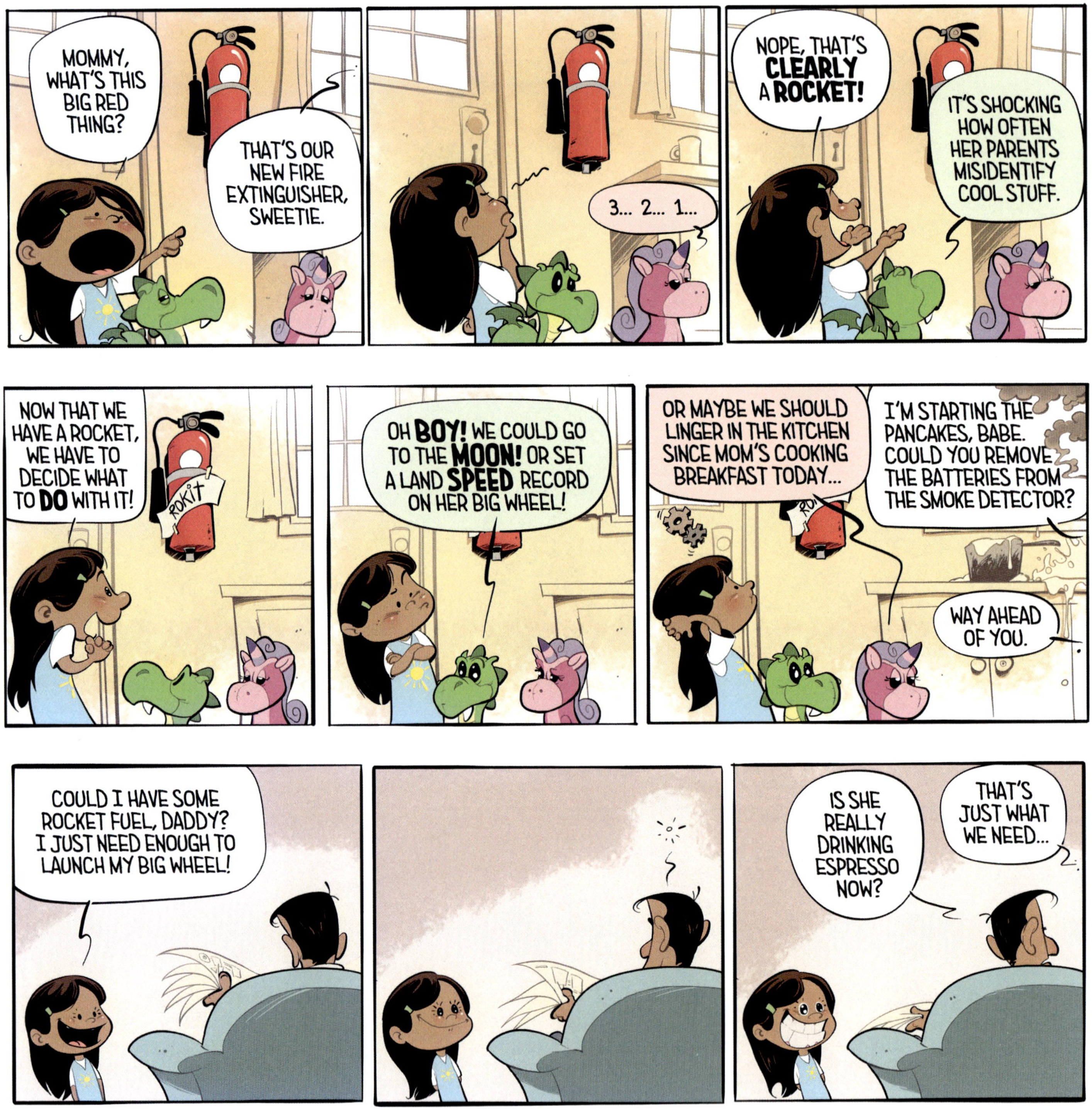
MOMMY, WHAT'S THIS BIG RED THING?
THAT'S OUR NEW FIRE EXTINGUISHER, SWEETIE.
3... 2... 1...
NOPE, THAT'S CLEARLY A ROCKET!
IT'S SHOCKING HOW OFTEN HER PARENTS MISIDENTIFY COOL STUFF.
NOW THAT WE HAVE A ROCKET, WE HAVE TO DECIDE WHAT TO DO WITH IT!
ROKIT
OH BOY! WE COULD GO TO THE MOON! OR SET A LAND SPEED RECORD ON HER BIG WHEEL!
OR MAYBE WE SHOULD LINGER IN THE KITCHEN SINCE MOM'S COOKING BREAKFAST TODAY...
I'M STARTING THE PANCAKES, BABE. COULD YOU REMOVE THE BATTERIES FROM THE SMOKE DETECTOR?
WAY AHEAD OF YOU.
COULD I HAVE SOME ROCKET FUEL, DADDY? I JUST NEED ENOUGH TO LAUNCH MY BIG WHEEL!
IS SHE REALLY DRINKING ESPRESSO NOW?
THAT'S JUST WHAT WE NEED...

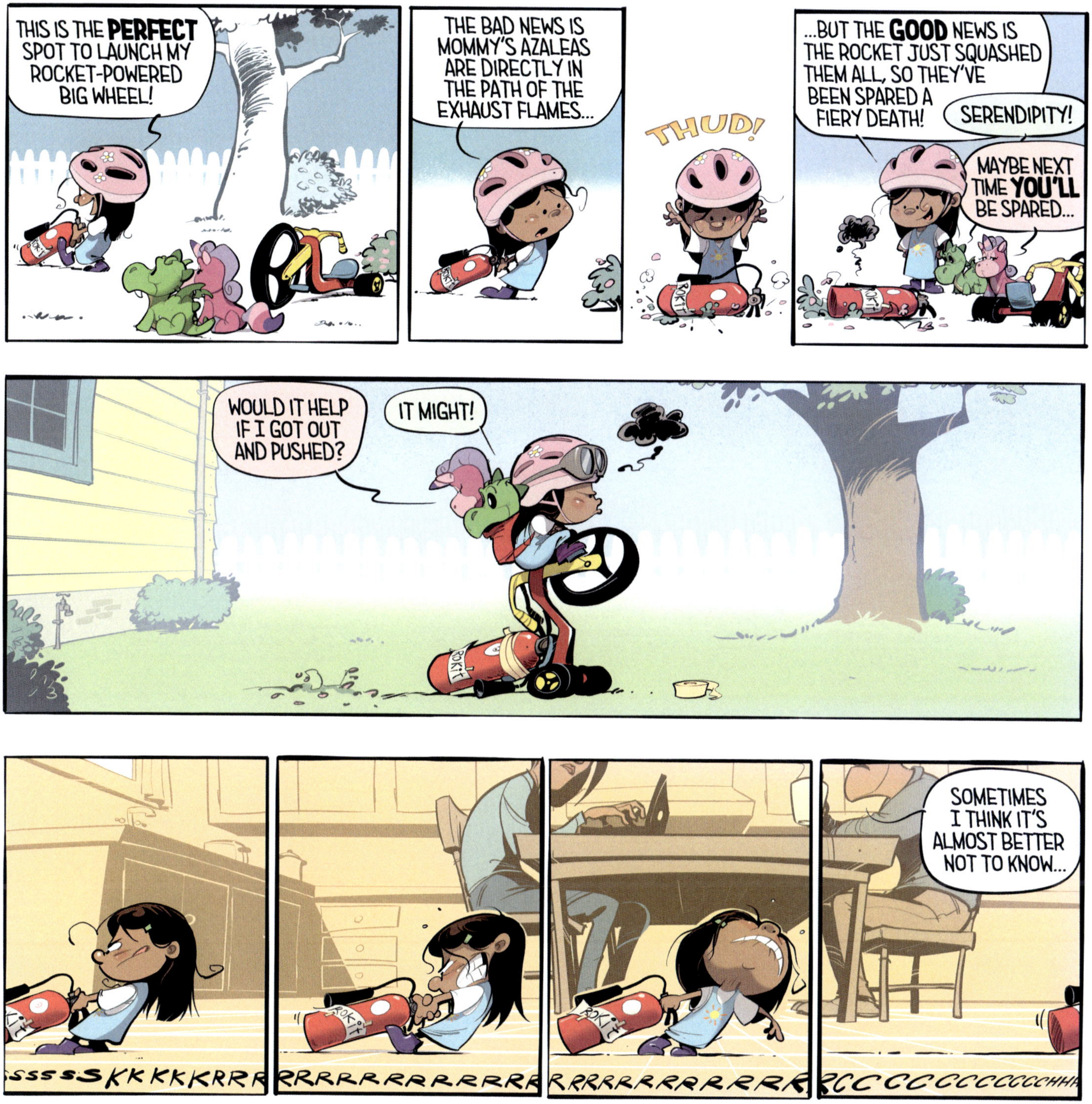
THIS IS THE **PERFECT** SPOT TO LAUNCH MY ROCKET-POWERED BIG WHEEL!
THE BAD NEWS IS MOMMY'S AZALEAS ARE DIRECTLY IN THE PATH OF THE EXHAUST FLAMES...
THUD!
...BUT THE **GOOD** NEWS IS THE ROCKET JUST SQUASHED THEM ALL, SO THEY'VE BEEN SPARED A FIERY DEATH!
SERENDIPITY!
MAYBE NEXT TIME **YOU'LL** BE SPARED...
WOULD IT HELP IF I GOT OUT AND PUSHED?
IT MIGHT!
SSSSSSKKKKKKRRR
RRRRRRRRRRRRRR
RRRRRRRRRRRRRR
RCCCCCCCCCCCCHHH
SOMETIMES I THINK IT'S ALMOST BETTER NOT TO KNOW...

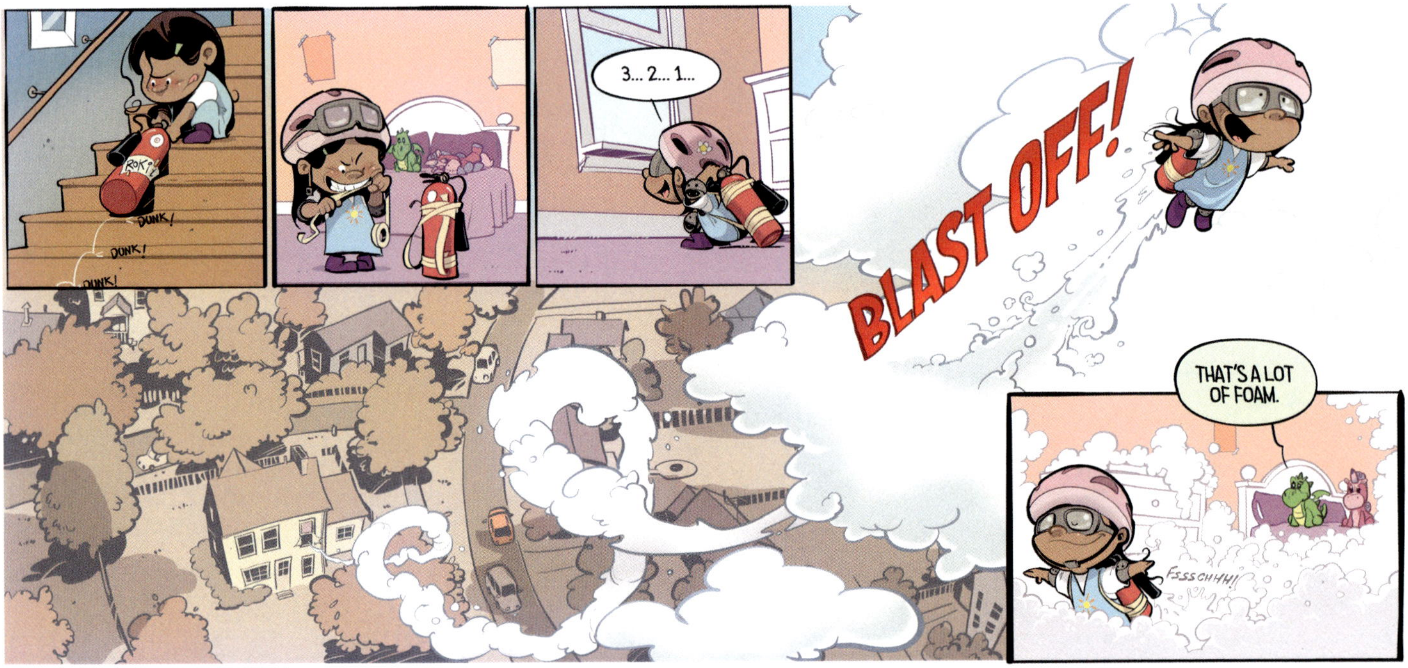
DUNK!
DUNK!
DUNK!
3... 2... 1...
BLAST OFF!
THAT'S A LOT OF FOAM.
FSSSCHHH!

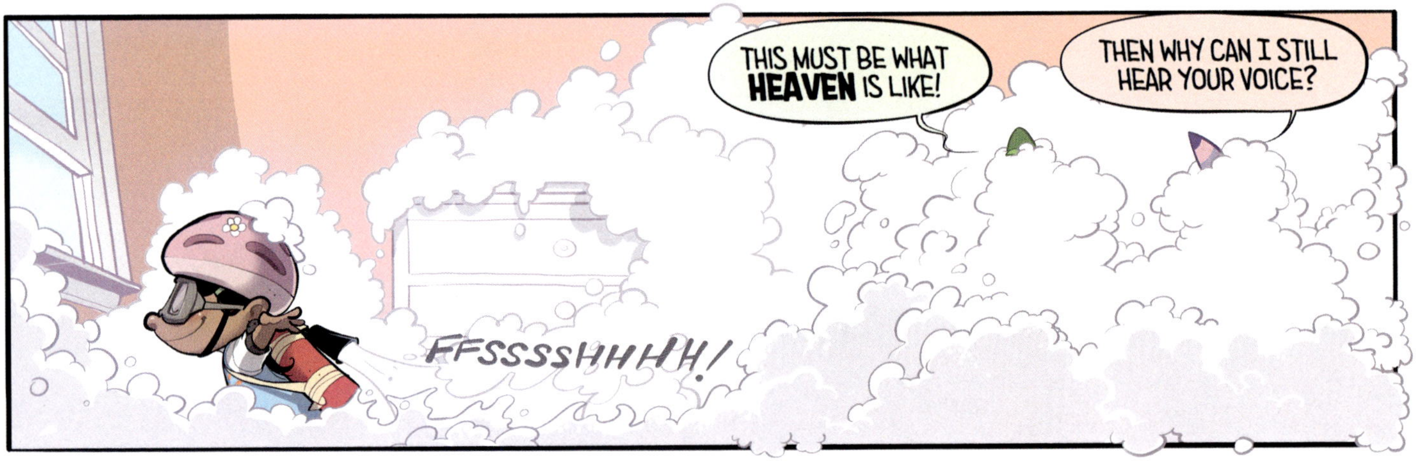
THIS MUST BE WHAT **HEAVEN** IS LIKE!
THEN WHY CAN I STILL HEAR YOUR VOICE?
FFSSSSHHHH!

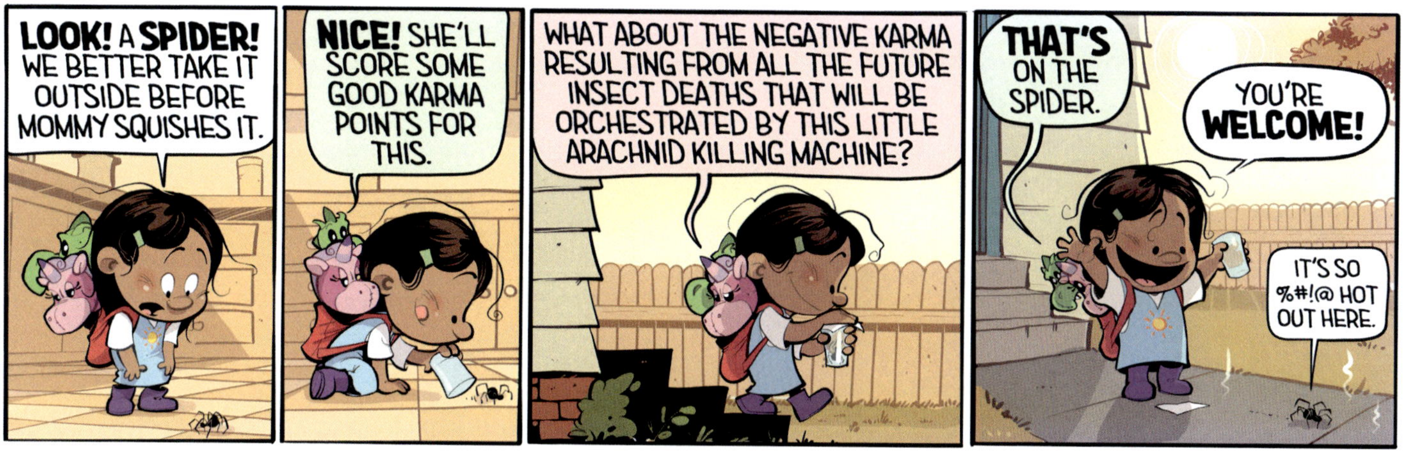
LOOK! A SPIDER! WE BETTER TAKE IT OUTSIDE BEFORE MOMMY SQUISHES IT.
NICE! SHE'LL SCORE SOME GOOD KARMA POINTS FOR THIS.
WHAT ABOUT THE NEGATIVE KARMA RESULTING FROM ALL THE FUTURE INSECT DEATHS THAT WILL BE ORCHESTRATED BY THIS LITTLE ARACHNID KILLING MACHINE?
THAT'S ON THE SPIDER.
YOU'RE WELCOME!
IT'S SO %#!@ HOT OUT HERE.

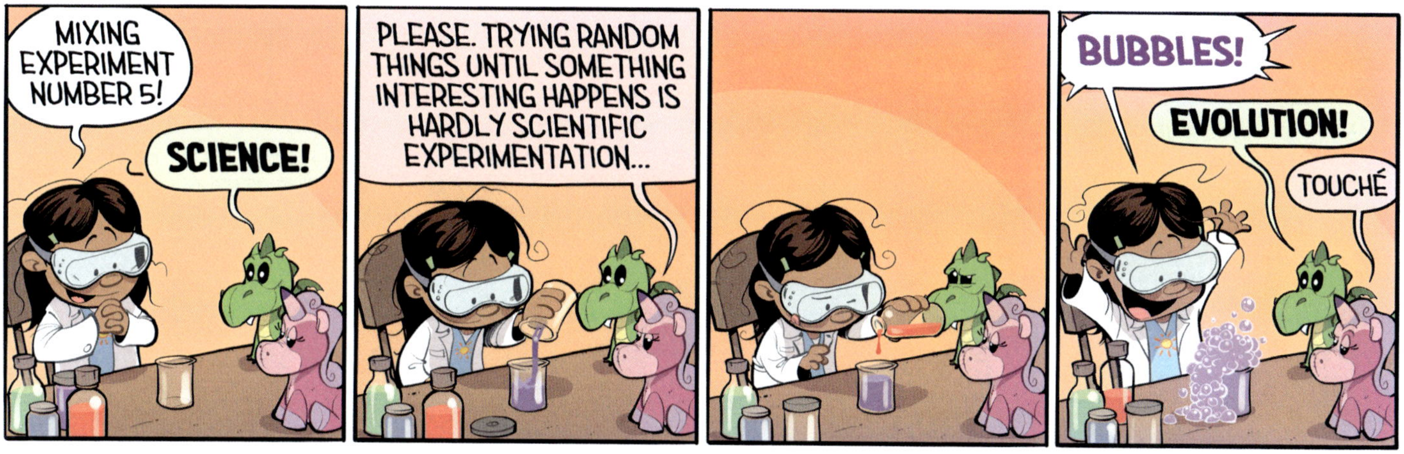
MIXING EXPERIMENT NUMBER 5!
SCIENCE!
PLEASE. TRYING RANDOM THINGS UNTIL SOMETHING INTERESTING HAPPENS IS HARDLY SCIENTIFIC EXPERIMENTATION...
BUBBLES!
EVOLUTION!
TOUCHÉ

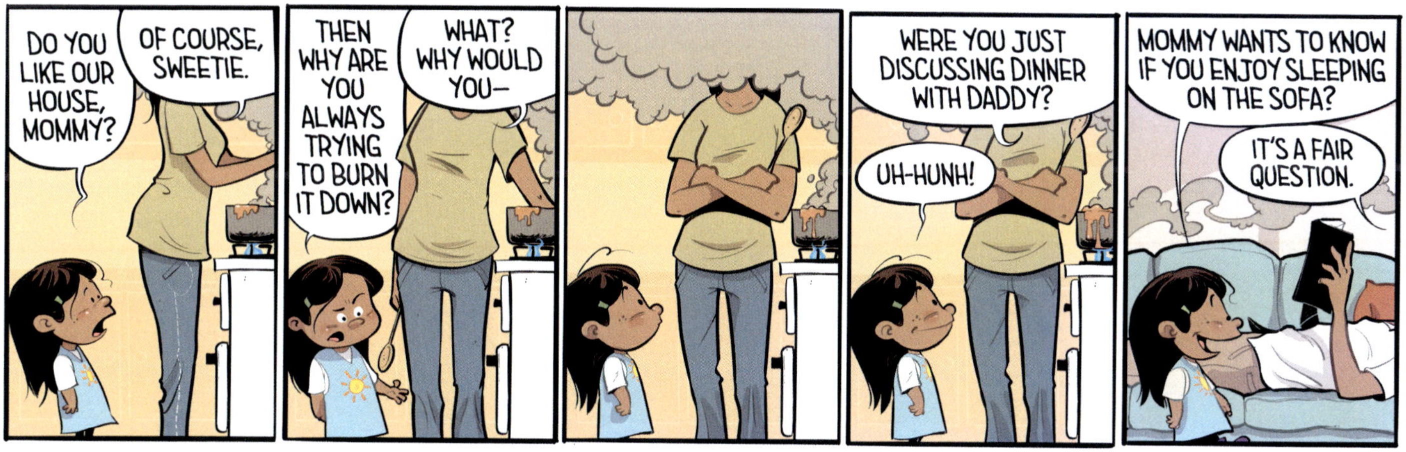
DO YOU LIKE OUR HOUSE, MOMMY?
OF COURSE, SWEETIE.
THEN WHY ARE YOU ALWAYS TRYING TO BURN IT DOWN?
WHAT? WHY WOULD YOU—
WERE YOU JUST DISCUSSING DINNER WITH DADDY?
UH-HUNH!
MOMMY WANTS TO KNOW IF YOU ENJOY SLEEPING ON THE SOFA?
IT'S A FAIR QUESTION.

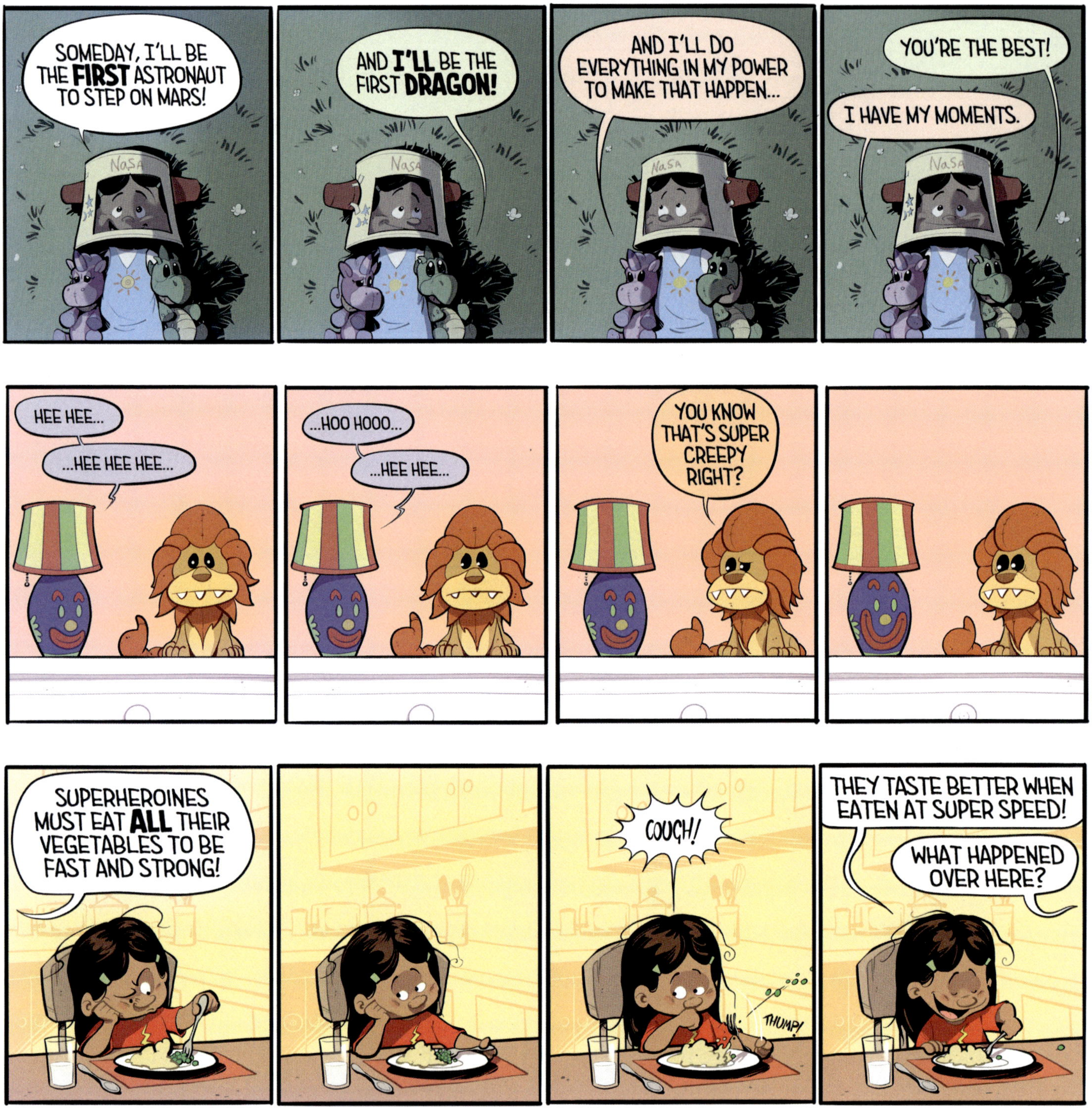
SOMEDAY, I'LL BE THE FIRST ASTRONAUT TO STEP ON MARS!
AND I'LL BE THE FIRST DRAGON!
AND I'LL DO EVERYTHING IN MY POWER TO MAKE THAT HAPPEN...
YOU'RE THE BEST!
I HAVE MY MOMENTS.
HEE HEE...
...HEE HEE HEE...
...HOO HOOO...
...HEE HEE...
YOU KNOW THAT'S SUPER CREEPY RIGHT?
SUPERHEROINES MUST EAT ALL THEIR VEGETABLES TO BE FAST AND STRONG!
COUGH!
THUMP!
THEY TASTE BETTER WHEN EATEN AT SUPER SPEED!
WHAT HAPPENED OVER HERE?

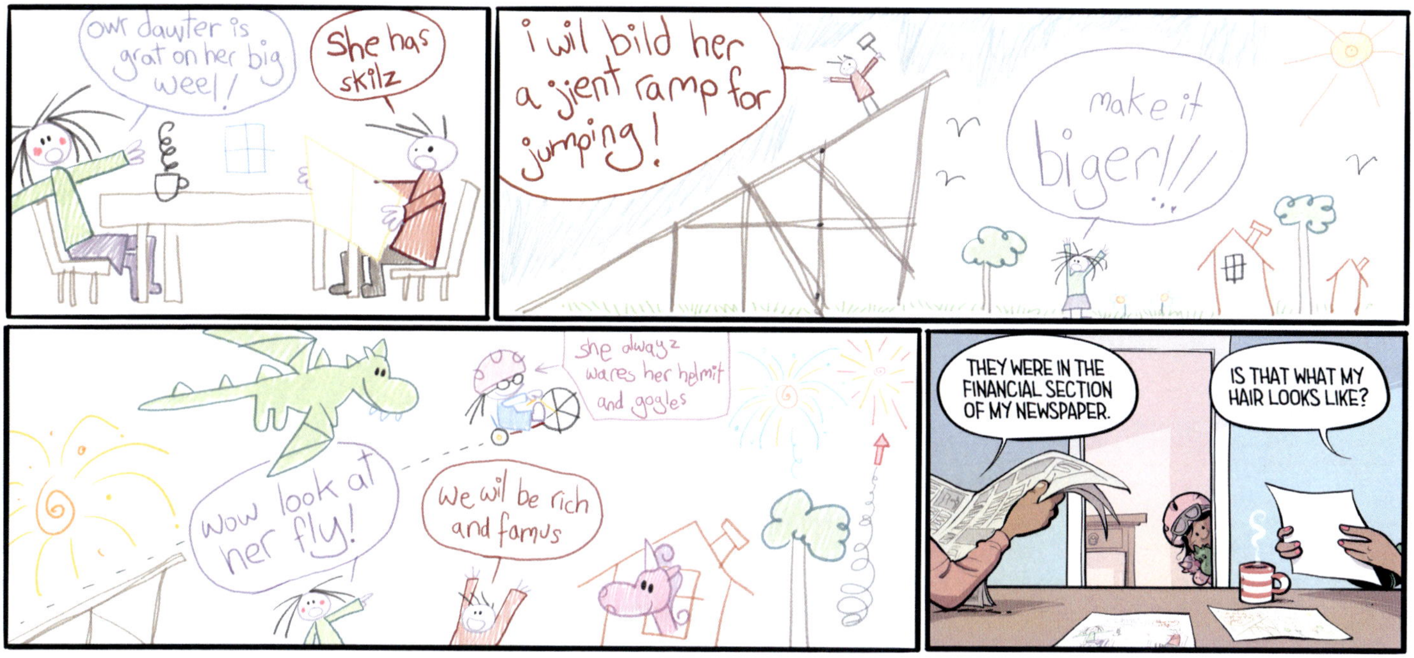
owr dawter is grat on her big weel!
She has skilz
i wil bild her a jient ramp for jumping!
make it biger!!!
she alwayz wares her helmit and gogles
wow look at her fly!
We wil be rich and famus
THEY WERE IN THE FINANCIAL SECTION OF MY NEWSPAPER.
IS THAT WHAT MY HAIR LOOKS LIKE?

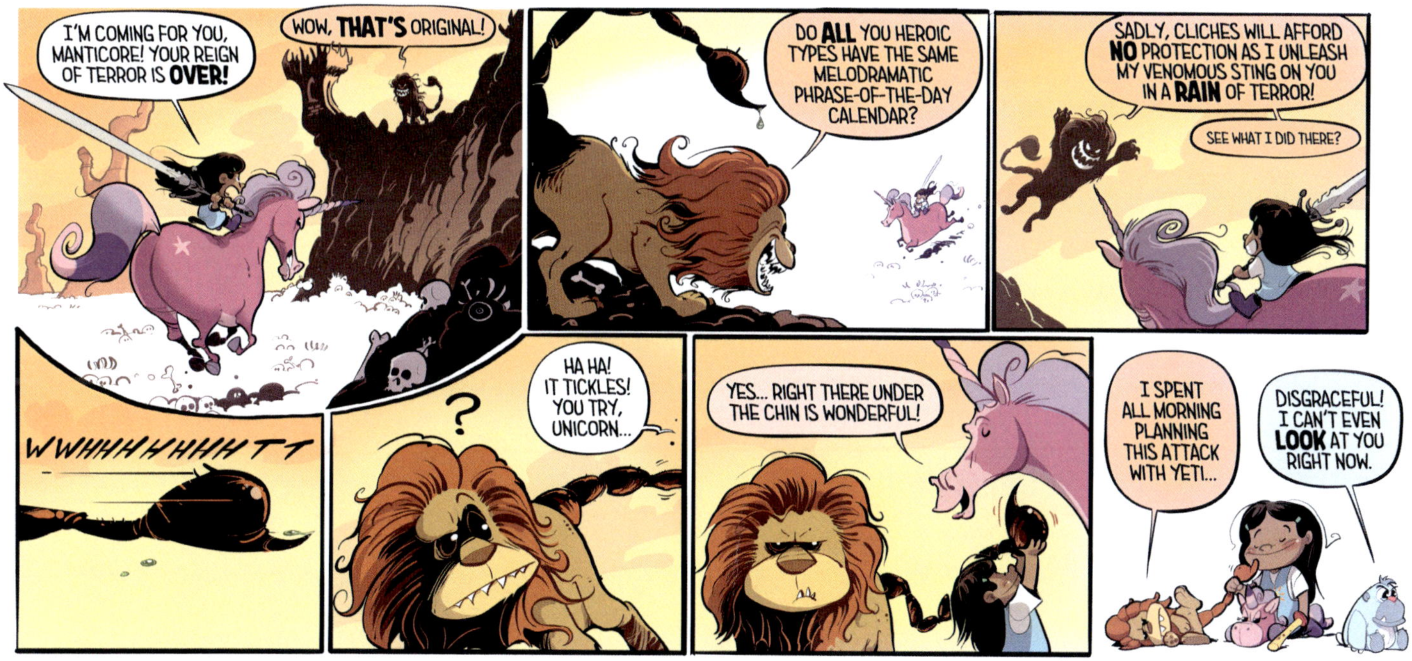
I'M COMING FOR YOU, MANTICORE! YOUR REIGN OF TERROR IS **OVER!**
WOW, **THAT'S** ORIGINAL!
DO **ALL** YOU HEROIC TYPES HAVE THE SAME MELODRAMATIC PHRASE-OF-THE-DAY CALENDAR?
SADLY, CLICHES WILL AFFORD **NO** PROTECTION AS I UNLEASH MY VENOMOUS STING ON YOU IN A **RAIN** OF TERROR!
SEE WHAT I DID THERE?
WWHHHHHHHHTT
?
HA HA! IT TICKLES! YOU TRY, UNICORN...
YES... RIGHT THERE UNDER THE CHIN IS WONDERFUL!
I SPENT ALL MORNING PLANNING THIS ATTACK WITH YETI...
DISGRACEFUL! I CAN'T EVEN **LOOK** AT YOU RIGHT NOW.

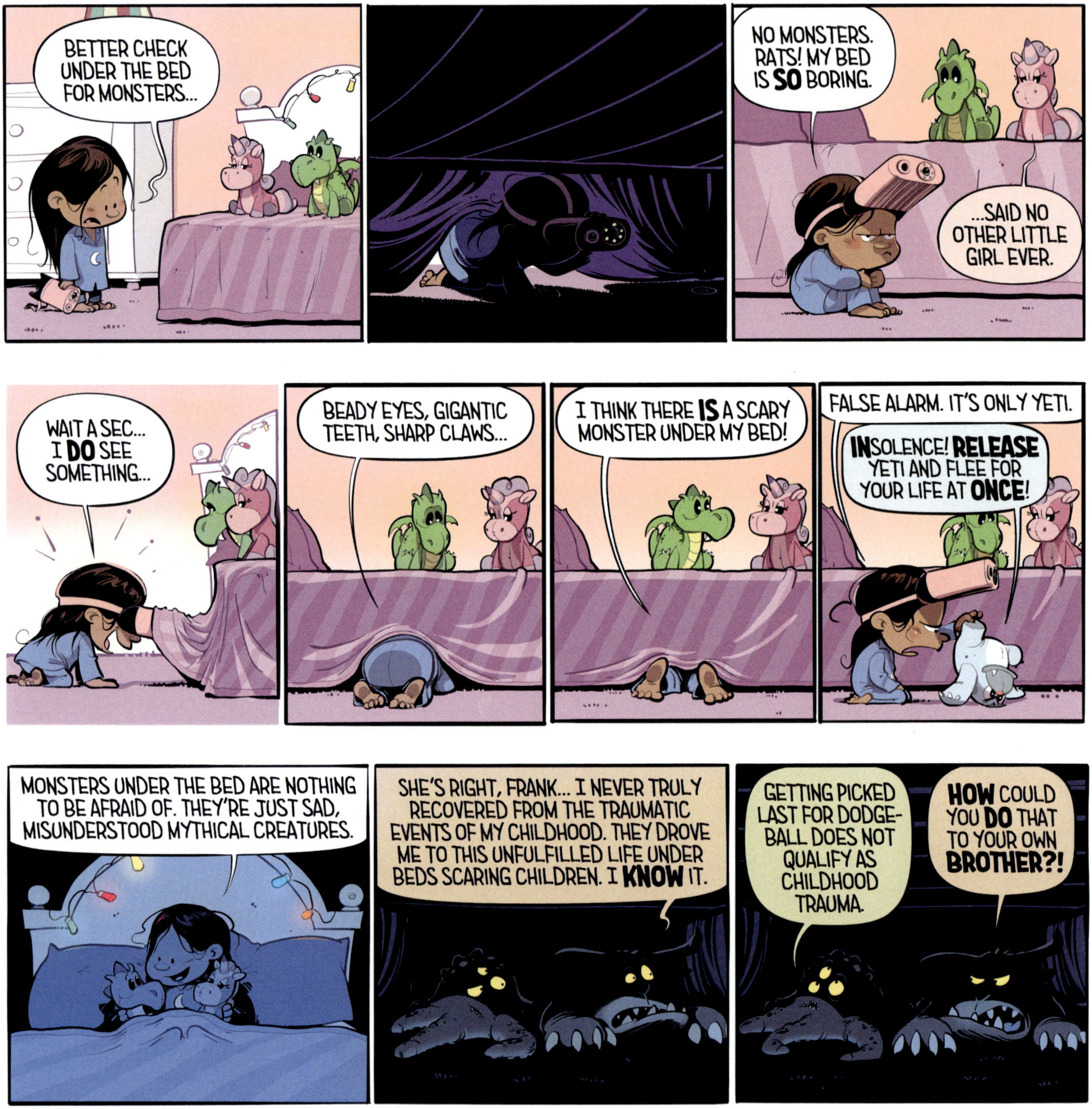
BETTER CHECK UNDER THE BED FOR MONSTERS...
NO MONSTERS. RATS! MY BED IS **SO** BORING.
...SAID NO OTHER LITTLE GIRL EVER.
WAIT A SEC... I **DO** SEE SOMETHING...
BEADY EYES, GIGANTIC TEETH, SHARP CLAWS...
I THINK THERE **IS** A SCARY MONSTER UNDER MY BED!
FALSE ALARM. IT'S ONLY YETI.
INSOLENCE! **RELEASE** YETI AND FLEE FOR YOUR LIFE AT **ONCE**!
MONSTERS UNDER THE BED ARE NOTHING TO BE AFRAID OF. THEY'RE JUST SAD, MISUNDERSTOOD MYTHICAL CREATURES.
SHE'S RIGHT, FRANK... I NEVER TRULY RECOVERED FROM THE TRAUMATIC EVENTS OF MY CHILDHOOD. THEY DROVE ME TO THIS UNFULFILLED LIFE UNDER BEDS SCARING CHILDREN. I **KNOW** IT.
GETTING PICKED LAST FOR DODGE-BALL DOES NOT QUALIFY AS CHILDHOOD TRAUMA.
HOW COULD YOU **DO** THAT TO YOUR OWN **BROTHER?!**

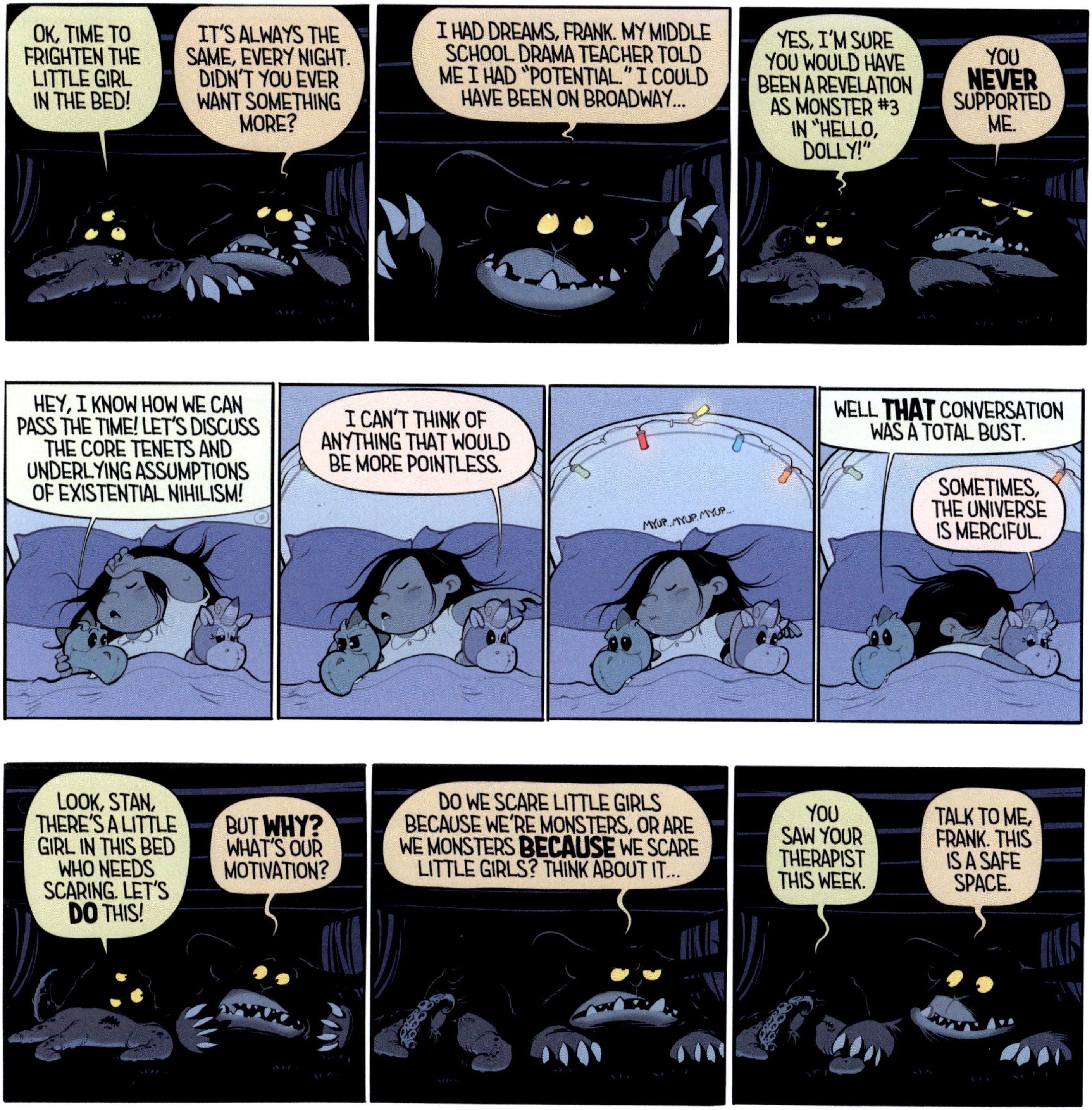
OK, TIME TO FRIGHTEN THE LITTLE GIRL IN THE BED!
IT'S ALWAYS THE SAME, EVERY NIGHT. DIDN'T YOU EVER WANT SOMETHING MORE?
I HAD DREAMS, FRANK. MY MIDDLE SCHOOL DRAMA TEACHER TOLD ME I HAD "POTENTIAL." I COULD HAVE BEEN ON BROADWAY...
YES, I'M SURE YOU WOULD HAVE BEEN A REVELATION AS MONSTER #3 IN "HELLO, DOLLY!"
YOU NEVER SUPPORTED ME.
HEY, I KNOW HOW WE CAN PASS THE TIME! LET'S DISCUSS THE CORE TENETS AND UNDERLYING ASSUMPTIONS OF EXISTENTIAL NIHILISM!
I CAN'T THINK OF ANYTHING THAT WOULD BE MORE POINTLESS.
MYUP..MYUP..MYUP...
WELL THAT CONVERSATION WAS A TOTAL BUST.
SOMETIMES, THE UNIVERSE IS MERCIFUL.
LOOK, STAN, THERE'S A LITTLE GIRL IN THIS BED WHO NEEDS SCARING. LET'S DO THIS!
BUT WHY? WHAT'S OUR MOTIVATION?
DO WE SCARE LITTLE GIRLS BECAUSE WE'RE MONSTERS, OR ARE WE MONSTERS BECAUSE WE SCARE LITTLE GIRLS? THINK ABOUT IT...
YOU SAW YOUR THERAPIST THIS WEEK.
TALK TO ME, FRANK. THIS IS A SAFE SPACE.

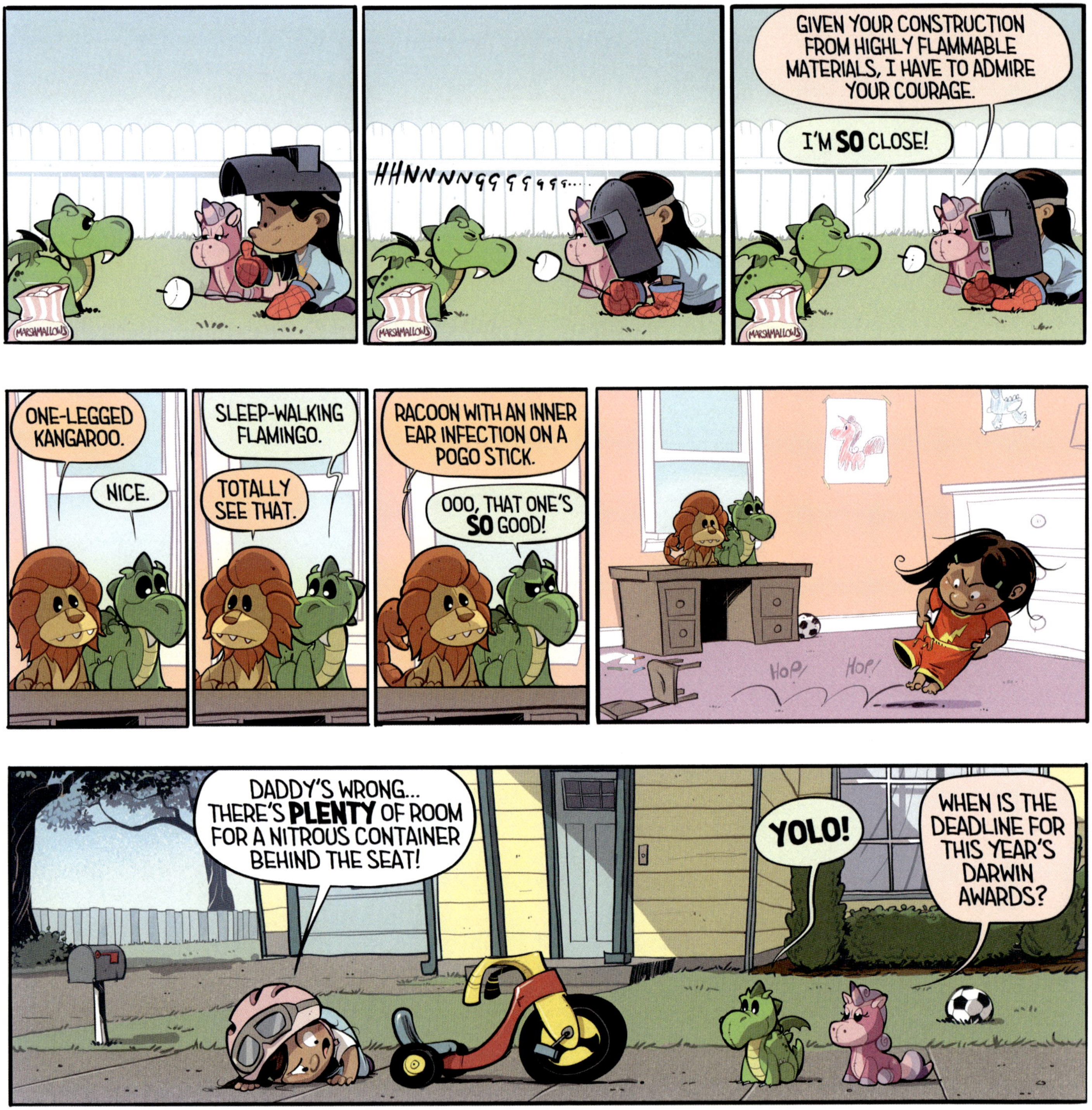
MARSHMALLOWS
HHNNNNGGGGGGG....
GIVEN YOUR CONSTRUCTION FROM HIGHLY FLAMMABLE MATERIALS, I HAVE TO ADMIRE YOUR COURAGE.
I'M **SO** CLOSE!
ONE-LEGGED KANGAROO.
NICE.
SLEEP-WALKING FLAMINGO.
TOTALLY SEE THAT.
RACOON WITH AN INNER EAR INFECTION ON A POGO STICK.
OOO, THAT ONE'S **SO** GOOD!
HOP! HOP!
DADDY'S WRONG... THERE'S **PLENTY** OF ROOM FOR A NITROUS CONTAINER BEHIND THE SEAT!
YOLO!
WHEN IS THE DEADLINE FOR THIS YEAR'S DARWIN AWARDS?

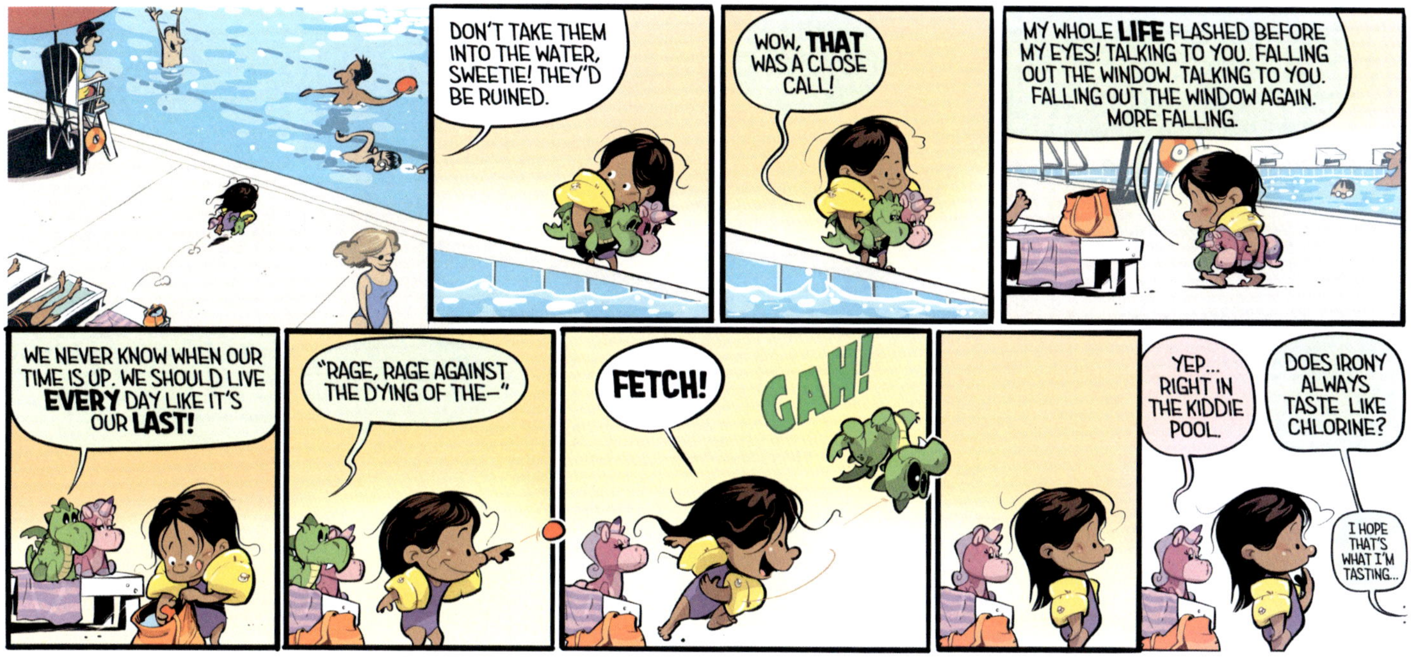
DON'T TAKE THEM INTO THE WATER, SWEETIE! THEY'D BE RUINED.
WOW, THAT WAS A CLOSE CALL!
MY WHOLE LIFE FLASHED BEFORE MY EYES! TALKING TO YOU. FALLING OUT THE WINDOW. TALKING TO YOU. FALLING OUT THE WINDOW AGAIN. MORE FALLING.
WE NEVER KNOW WHEN OUR TIME IS UP. WE SHOULD LIVE EVERY DAY LIKE IT'S OUR LAST!
"RAGE, RAGE AGAINST THE DYING OF THE–"
FETCH!
GAH!
YEP... RIGHT IN THE KIDDIE POOL.
DOES IRONY ALWAYS TASTE LIKE CHLORINE?
I HOPE THAT'S WHAT I'M TASTING...

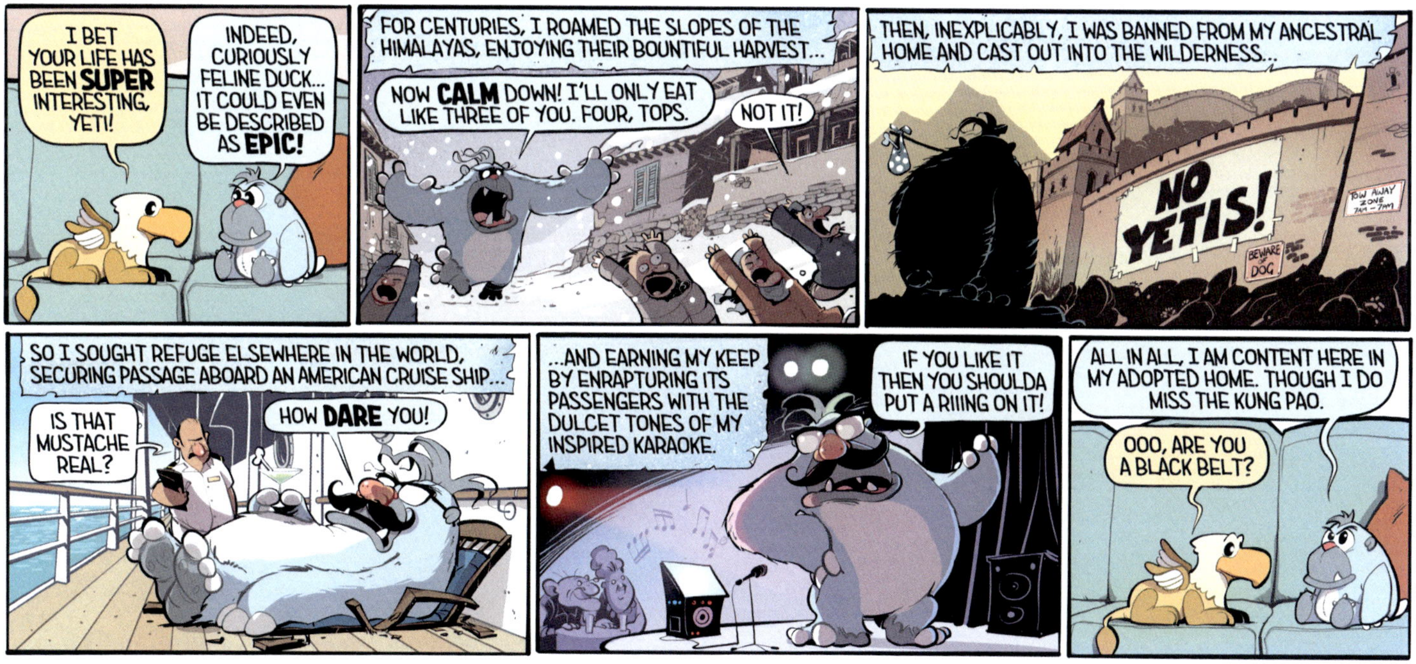
I BET YOUR LIFE HAS BEEN SUPER INTERESTING, YETI!
INDEED, CURIOUSLY FELINE DUCK... IT COULD EVEN BE DESCRIBED AS EPIC!
FOR CENTURIES, I ROAMED THE SLOPES OF THE HIMALAYAS, ENJOYING THEIR BOUNTIFUL HARVEST...
NOW CALM DOWN! I'LL ONLY EAT LIKE THREE OF YOU. FOUR, TOPS.
NOT IT!
THEN, INEXPLICABLY, I WAS BANNED FROM MY ANCESTRAL HOME AND CAST OUT INTO THE WILDERNESS...
NO YETIS!
TOW AWAY ZONE
BEWARE OF DOG
SO I SOUGHT REFUGE ELSEWHERE IN THE WORLD, SECURING PASSAGE ABOARD AN AMERICAN CRUISE SHIP...
IS THAT MUSTACHE REAL?
HOW DARE YOU!
...AND EARNING MY KEEP BY ENRAPTURING ITS PASSENGERS WITH THE DULCET TONES OF MY INSPIRED KARAOKE.
IF YOU LIKE IT THEN YOU SHOULDA PUT A RIIING ON IT!
ALL IN ALL, I AM CONTENT HERE IN MY ADOPTED HOME. THOUGH I DO MISS THE KUNG PAO.
OOO, ARE YOU A BLACK BELT?

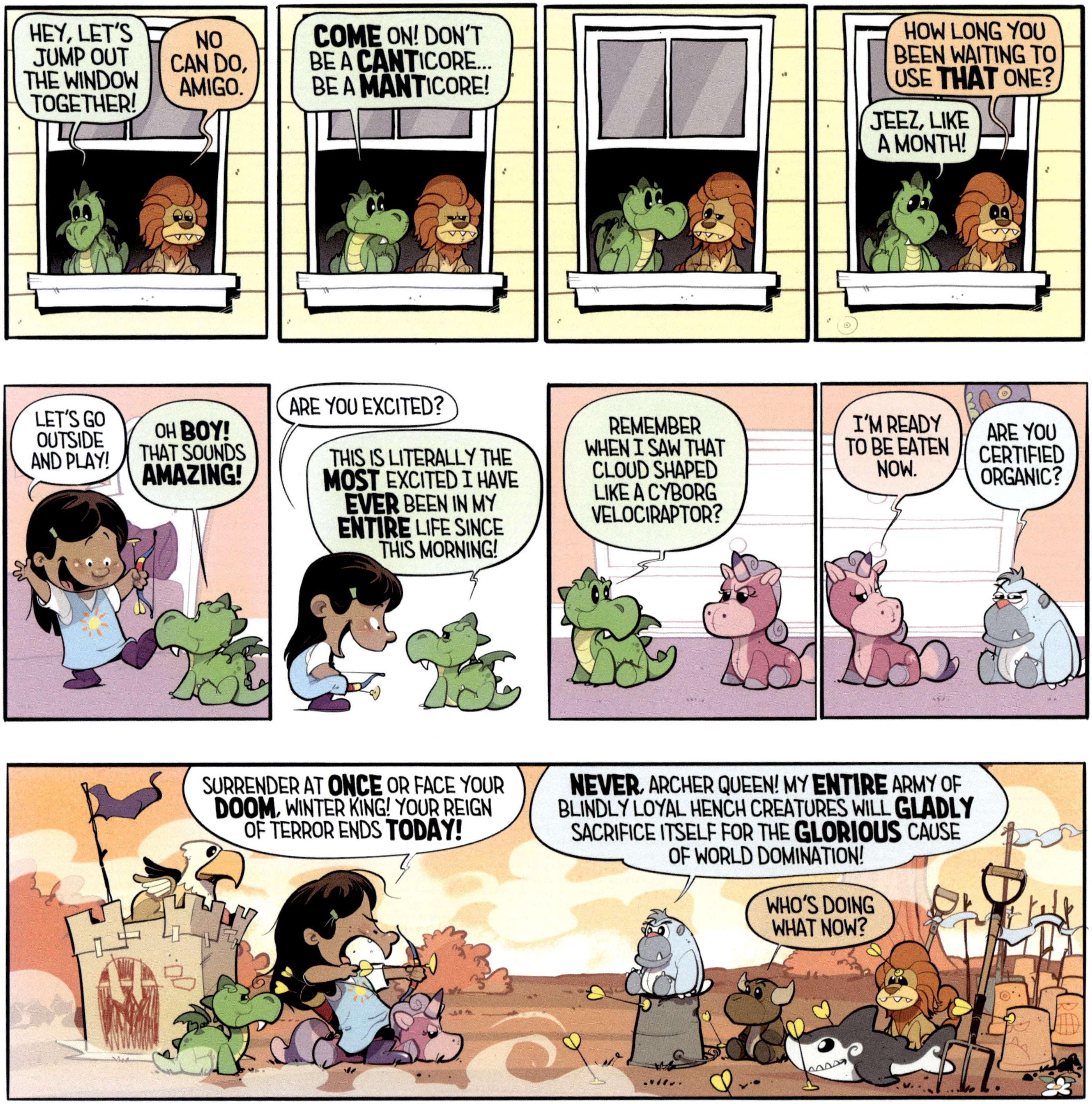
HEY, LET'S JUMP OUT THE WINDOW TOGETHER!
NO CAN DO, AMIGO.
COME ON! DON'T BE A CANTICORE... BE A MANTICORE!
HOW LONG YOU BEEN WAITING TO USE THAT ONE?
JEEZ, LIKE A MONTH!
LET'S GO OUTSIDE AND PLAY!
OH BOY! THAT SOUNDS AMAZING!
ARE YOU EXCITED?
THIS IS LITERALLY THE MOST EXCITED I HAVE EVER BEEN IN MY ENTIRE LIFE SINCE THIS MORNING!
REMEMBER WHEN I SAW THAT CLOUD SHAPED LIKE A CYBORG VELOCIRAPTOR?
I'M READY TO BE EATEN NOW.
ARE YOU CERTIFIED ORGANIC?
SURRENDER AT ONCE OR FACE YOUR DOOM, WINTER KING! YOUR REIGN OF TERROR ENDS TODAY!
NEVER, ARCHER QUEEN! MY ENTIRE ARMY OF BLINDLY LOYAL HENCH CREATURES WILL GLADLY SACRIFICE ITSELF FOR THE GLORIOUS CAUSE OF WORLD DOMINATION!
WHO'S DOING WHAT NOW?

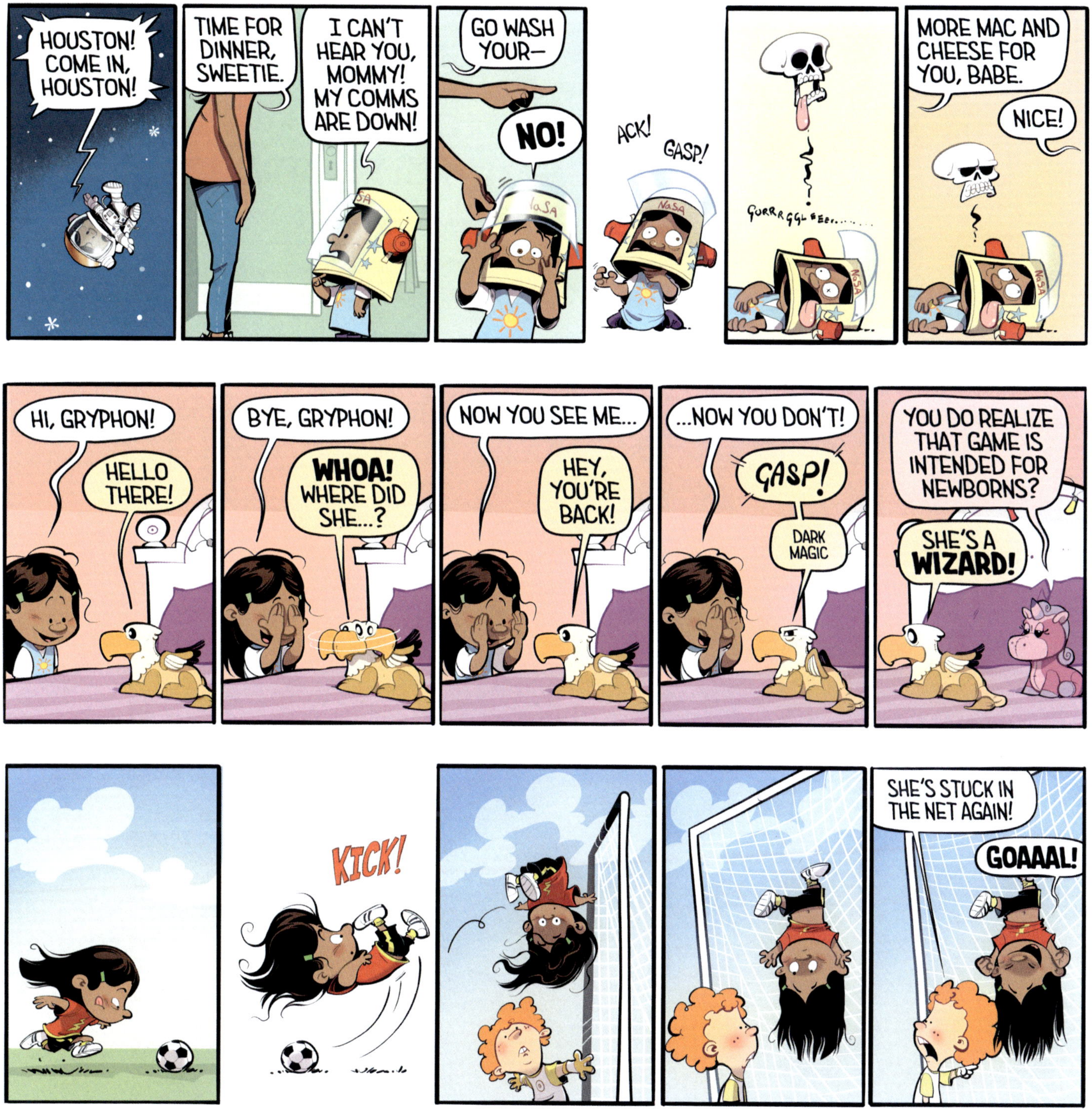
HOUSTON! COME IN, HOUSTON!
TIME FOR DINNER, SWEETIE.
I CAN'T HEAR YOU, MOMMY! MY COMMS ARE DOWN!
GO WASH YOUR—
NO!
ACK!
GASP!
GURRRRGGLEEE......
MORE MAC AND CHEESE FOR YOU, BABE.
NICE!
HI, GRYPHON!
HELLO THERE!
BYE, GRYPHON!
WHOA! WHERE DID SHE...?
NOW YOU SEE ME...
HEY, YOU'RE BACK!
...NOW YOU DON'T!
GASP!
DARK MAGIC
YOU DO REALIZE THAT GAME IS INTENDED FOR NEWBORNS?
SHE'S A WIZARD!
KICK!
SHE'S STUCK IN THE NET AGAIN!
GOAAAL!

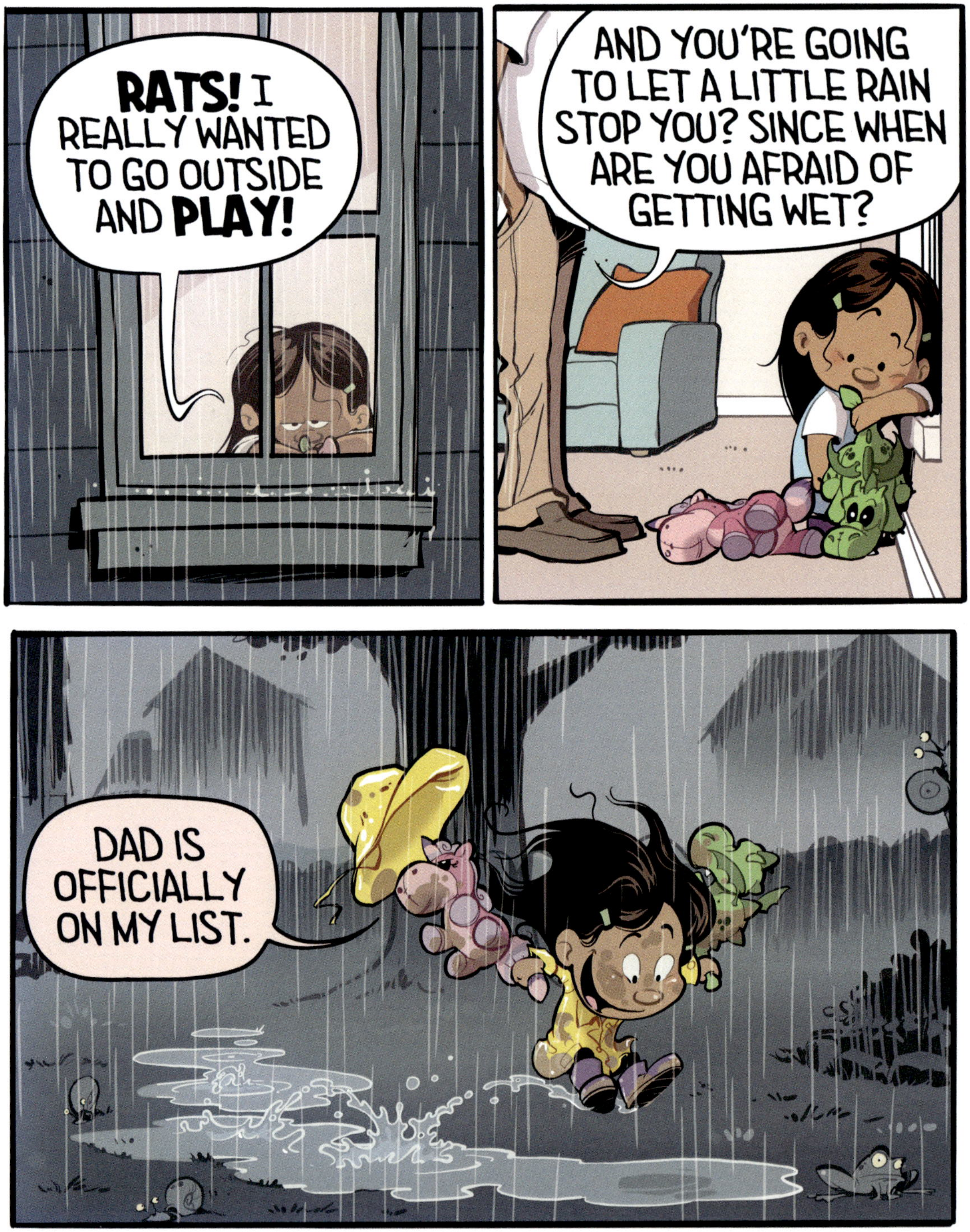

RATS! I REALLY WANTED TO GO OUTSIDE AND PLAY!
AND YOU'RE GOING TO LET A LITTLE RAIN STOP YOU? SINCE WHEN ARE YOU AFRAID OF GETTING WET?
DAD IS OFFICIALLY ON MY LIST.

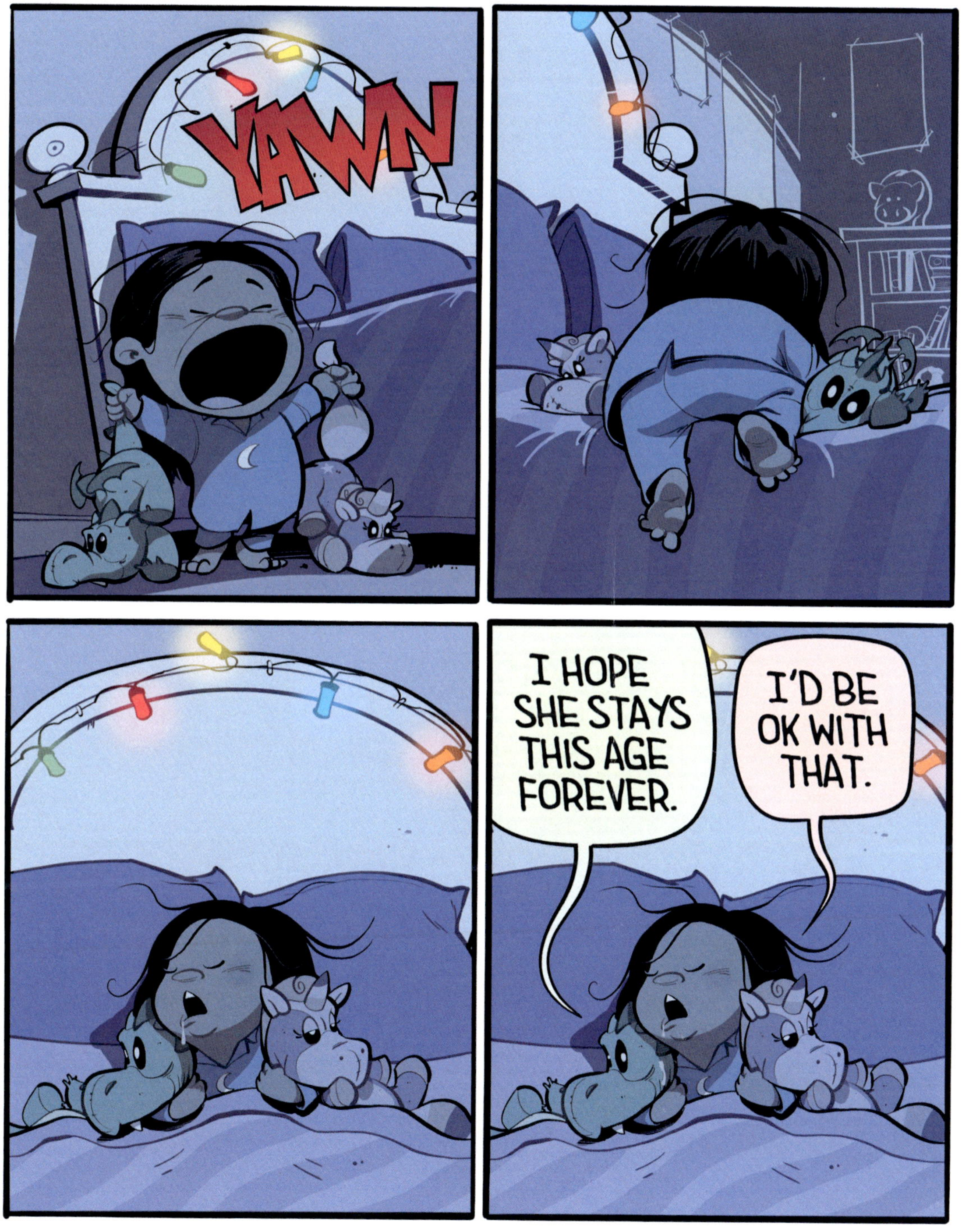
YAWN
I HOPE SHE STAYS THIS AGE FOREVER.
I'D BE OK WITH THAT.

 WWW.STUFFEDTHECOMIC.COM

 PATREON.COM/STUFFEDTHECOMIC

 FACEBOOK.COM/STUFFEDTHECOMIC

 @STUFFEDTHECOMIC

 @STUFFEDTHECOMIC

 WEBTOONS.COM SEARCH:"STUFFED"